Chicago's Neighboring South Shore
LAKE COUNTY
INDIANA

by **ARCHIBALD McKINLAY**

THE
DONNING COMPANY
PUBLISHERS

The Donning Company Publishers
184 Business Park Drive, Suite 206
Virginia Beach, VA 23462

Steve Mull, General Manager
Ed Williams, Project Director
Debbie Williams, Project Research Coordinator
Dawn V. Kofroth, Assistant General Manager
Sally C. Davis, Editor
Kelly M. Perkoski, Senior Graphic Designer
Marshall Rouse McClure, Graphic Designer
John Harrell, Imaging Artist
Scott Rule, Senior Marketing Coordinator
Patricia Peterson, Marketing Assistant

Library of Congress Cataloging-in-Publication Data
McKinlay, Archibald.
    Chicago's Neighboring South Shore : Lake County, Indiana / by Archibald McKinlay.
        p. cm.
        Includes index.
        ISBN 1–57864–102–0 (alk. paper)
        1. Lake County (Ind.)—Civilization. 2. Lake County (Ind.)—Pictorial Works. 3. Lake County (Ind.)—History, Local.
    F532.L2 M39 2001
    977.2'99—dc21
                                                            2001017252

Printed in Hong Kong

contents

dedication • 6

acknowledgments • 8

chapter 1
overview • 10

chapter 2
people • 16

chapter 3
work • 36

chapter 4
play • 54

chapter 5
parks • 80

chapter 6
amusements • 100

chapter 7
arts • 124

chapter 8
education • 136

chapter 9
community glimpses • 148

chapter 10
laureates • 162

index • 172

about the author • 176

dedication

To George Washington Clarke, who had a dream about Lake County, and backed it with gold.

George Washington Clarke came to Chicago from Brownsville, Pennsylvania in 1833 to help survey the Illinois and Michigan Canal. Through his work, he became acquainted with the Calumet River, one of five feeder rivers for the canal, and saw the territory's potential. During the California Gold Rush, he sailed a boatload of portable houses and other buildings around Cape Horn and, through middlemen, traded them to shelter-starved Forty Niners for gold dust. He then returned to Chicago and bought from the state of Indiana what had been classified as swampland; he also bought land through private sales and at sheriff tax sales. Between 1854 and 1861, he bought 19,549 acres, much of it in Lake County.

acknowledgments

To capture *Chicago's Neighboring South Shore: Lake County, Indiana*, I have been fortunate to have a number of allies who provided information and photographs. The basic source was *The Times*, a daily newspaper printed in Munster that has been named the best newspaper in Indiana five straight years. I especially owe a debt to Matt Mansfield, assistant managing editor, who opened the door to the paper's photo plunderhouse, and to Theresa Badovich, features editor. Thanks, too, to Bill Nangle, executive editor, who let it all happen, and to William E. Howard, publisher.

I'm also indebted to Geoffrey Black, head photographer, and Marlene Patterson, who is trying to systematize photos that are now largely digitized. Of critical importance, of course, are *The Times'* photographers themselves, including: Zbigniew Bzdak, Aldino Gallo, Brett Reierson, Tracy Albano, Sam Riche, Gregg Gearhart, Mike Gard, Natalie Battaglia, Yvette Marie Dostatni, John J. Watkins, and Wes Pope, in addition to Geoffrey Black.

I also owe much to Linda Dorman-Gainer of the Northern Indiana Arts Association, who headed the PhotoCalumet project that comprised fifteen photographers who each shot a different aspect of Lake County. Some of these photos are in this book, including a few taken by Linda herself. I also owe a great deal to Marcia Carle, proprietor of Carle Communications, arguably the top public relations firm in Northwest Indiana. Marcia came up with a gallery of outstanding photos on the city of Hammond. And thanks to Art Schweizter, who has photo-documented every facet of Schererville and Dyer, and who contributed key photos to this book. Likewise Gayle Kosalko, who knows just about all there is to know about Whiting/Robertsdale, and who also contributed important information and photos. And thanks to Tom Hocker, a great talent; Joanna Shearer, the eyes of the Lake County Park system; and just plain Alan, who is always in the neighborhood when a special photographic touch is needed. Other photographers and sources, like Paul A. Meyers, are credited in the captions of their photographs.

Then there's Richard D. "Dick" Rudzinski, for many years the head photographer of *The Times*, who came out of retirement to give me a hand. Some years ago, during a mid-life crisis, Dick gave up photography in favor of running charter fishing boats on Lake Michigan. When an injury sidelined him, he exchanged his captain's hat for a walking stick. Nevertheless, while leaning on a cane with one hand and clicking his trusty camera with the other, he captured some of the scenes you'll see in the pages ahead. Dick is still one of the best photographers going, and the gamest.

On the artistic side, special thanks to Al Odlivak, whom I call the Norman Rockwell of Whiting. Using scraps of material, like pieces of masonite, Al has virtually painted the history of Whiting/Robertsdale. Although he works from photographs, each Odlivak creation is decidedly an original work of art that captures a feeling of Lake County in a way photographs cannot. I have used a sampling of his delightful paintings in this book.

When photographic gaps had to be filled, my wife, Patricia Young McKinlay, whose day job is being senior vice president of Resurrection Health Care in Chicago, stepped in with a good eye and sure shot. She also critiqued and edited the manuscript for the book. So, I thank her too, although I thank her so often every day for all the things she does for me that my thank-you's sound almost insincere. They are not.

And a last-minute note of gratitude. After this book was all but completed, I became aware that John Davies, then marketing vice president of the Northwest Indiana Forum, was riding a brilliant idea into orbit. Using the famous 1920s South Shore posters, which you've probably seen advertised in national catalogs, he directed a group of artists in the creation of a Millennium Series of posters that appropriates the look of the old posters while illustrating present-day subjects. I have tried to fit a smattering of these increasingly popular posters into the present book.

—*Archibald McKinlay*
Chicago, Illinois

chapter 1

Diversity, Diversity, Diversity

If Lake County, Indiana, had to be reduced to one word, that word would be DIVERSITY.

It is diverse almost beyond imagination in virtually every facet of human life. Lake County is especially diverse in the peoples who populate it. After 1833 when President Andrew Jackson bade all native Americans to hie themselves west of the Mississippi River, westering folk from the East replaced the Potawatomi. Close on their heels came the English, and when the floodgates of Germany opened shortly thereafter, the county became predominantly Teutonic.

Indeed, St. John Township, first settled by John Hack in 1837, was virtually all German, and Hanover Township, settled in 1838 by Henry Sasse, Henry Von Hollen, and Lewis Herlitz, became not only dominated by Germans but Germans from Hanover, Germany. Even here there was diversity. St. John's Township was practically entirely German Catholic, while Hanover Township was almost entirely German Lutheran. Since those early days, virtually every hue and strain on the planet has taken up residence in Lake County where, after several generations, they have become a unique blend of the old world and the new.

Lake County's legendary industry, too, is about as diverse as it gets, ranging from steel-making to electric-power brokering. Yet, the county is still an important producer of food and food products, and is a universal user of computers and other high technology. Among service industries, healthcare has emerged as the chief employer in several cities of Lake County, and its hospitals are among the most up-to-date in the Midwest.

The diversity of recreation begins with Lake County's matchless beaches, both on Lake Michigan and on inland lakes. In addition to swimming and fishing, sailing has surfaced as a popular recreation, especially since the creation of two world-class marinas on The Big Lake. Moreover, eleven highly-diverse county parks have taken root to complement a huge township park and the fine parks of individual cities. And, of course, there is golf. Players can choose from a range of courses suited to their skills, whether hacker or scratch golfer.

overview

As for diversions and amusements, no one spending time in Lake County is likely to be bored. Among the most popular diversions are four giant floating casinos that ply the waters of Lake Michigan. These spectacular pleasure crafts provide patrons with opportunities not only to rattle a pair of bones and spin a chancey wheel, but to be fed and entertained royally. For land-based stage shows, a complex in Merrillville attracts just about every big-name concert performer and band in the land, and an arts center in Munster presents plays and musicals by top-of-the-line road show companies. For the classically inclined, the Indiana Symphony Orchestra makes the best music sound better, including pops music, and for the sports minded. . . . well, nothing beats Indiana basketball.

In recent years, Lake County has also become a center for quality education of all varieties at all levels, and for specialized museums and archives that attract scholars and visitors of various stripes. Few places can match the depth of historical information in the East Chicago Room, the Calumet Room (Hammond), or the Regional Archives of Indiana University Northwest (Gary). Nor are there many towns with a local history museum as comprehensive as the one in Hobart.

In the pages that follow, all of this and more is set in a historical context that is unique among American counties, each diversified unit of the county being its own object of fascination.

In what were recently cornfields, one will today find Old World cathedrals, such as Merrillville's Saints Constantine and Helen Cathedral, shown here. Photo courtesy of the Lake County Convention and Visitors Bureau.

Among many amusements found in Lake County, one of the most popular is casino gaming on so-called river boats, four of which ply Lake Michigan waters in Lake County. Photo courtesy of the Lake County Convention and Visitors Bureau.

A truly unique tour is sometimes offered by LTV Steel. With advance scheduling, individuals are formed into groups and taken through the stages of the steel-making process. LTV Steel Photo.

Sailing is as natural to Lake County as winds from the west, so there are several world-class marinas to serve recreational sailors. Times photo by Tracy Albano.

13

Most fine arts in Lake County are concentrated in the Center for Visual and Performing Arts in Munster. In addition, the Center provides many amenities, such as fine dining, tastefully designed exterior and interior, and beautiful grounds, enhanced here by Janie Wilson, a bonny lass who happens to be assistant general manager of the Center. Photo by Richard D. Rudzinski.

The last interurban line in America, the ninety-mile South Shore has an annual ridership of more than three million. It offers Lake County residents and visitors a quick ride to downtown Chicago. Times photo.

Surf and sun is abundantly available at six public beaches that line the county's Lake Michigan coast. Photo courtesy of the Lake County Convention and Visitors Bureau.

Lake County has experienced a hotel and motel explosion that shows no signs of abating. In all, more than three thousand hotel rooms fill a variety of needs. Photo courtesy of the Lake County Convention and Visitors Bureau.

chapter 2

The Ultimate Melting Pot

More than a hundred races and nationalities mingle freely and harmoniously within the bounds of Lake County, America's ultimate melting pot. For a century and two-thirds, this mixture of cultures has been constantly changing with the addition of new ingredients, slowing fusing and becoming Americanized in a unique unity that preserves ethnic identities.

After being populated for two-thirds of a century by native white Americans and northern Europeans known as the "Old Immigration," Lake County received, in the late-nineteenth century, massive infusions of people from central, eastern, and southern Europe and Asia Minor—the "New Immigration." A special census conducted by the North Township Trustee in 1907 found that eighty-five percent of all residents of the new town (1901) of Indiana Harbor were foreign-born; as were seventy-five percent of East Chicago's residents, fifty percent of Hammond's, and fifty percent of Whiting's. Until World War I, most people in the county's industrial north spoke English as a second language.

After several generations of Americanization, and especially since World War II, many residents of the north slid southward and mixed with less exotic Americans, many descended from settlers from the East and South, many others from German immigrants. Today, the population throughout Lake County is a diverse admixture of races and nationalities, each retaining at least a trace of its ethnic heritage, and sometimes a good deal more. And time, training, and education have brought with them new skills for these blended peoples, who constitute one of America's most productive and ablest workforces, and one of its solid rocks of citizenship.

At the start of a new millennium, most people in Lake County were alloyed-Americans, strong and durable, yet flexible and decidedly well-trained and well-educated. Blue collar in heritage and values, but thoroughly modern in outlook, the well-grounded, unaffected, congenial people of Lake County are about as real as people can be.

people

Echoes of distant cultures resonate in Lake County's almost non-stop festivals. Here a Slovak dance troop participates in Whiting's annual Pierogi Fest. Photo courtesy of the Whiting Chamber of Commerce.

Today's Lake County residents keep in touch with that part of their Native American heritage by means of special presentations by traveling Native Americans, such as the one shown here. Photo by Tom Hocker.

In recent years, a resurgence of interest in Irish dancing has not been lost on Lake County. Here (left to right) dancers Kathleen Killen, Erin Kalisz, and Annie Doody perform in Merrillville at a St. Patrick's Day event. *Times* photo by Tracy Albano.

Hammond's International Culture Festival in early September does not exclude the strictly American. Photo by Patricia Young McKinlay.

Displays of peasants in native costumes can be found in several of the museums of Lake County. Photo by Tom Hocker.

The cultures of most ethnic groups in Lake County usually include an emphasis on singing. Photo by Tom Hocker.

Tasty by-products of Latino influxes are a variety of restaurants that fit all tastes and budgets. At the culinary high end of the scale is the beautiful Casa Blanca restaurant in East Chicago, shown here, which faithfully follows the architectural traditions of the finest restaurants in Mexico, even to the imported stone and tile. Photo by Tom Hocker.

The densest concentration of Slovaks was in Whiting/Robertsdale, where thousands of them worked at the Standard Oil (BP Amoco) refinery. To accommodate these men and their families, St. John the Baptist Church was established in Robertsdale in 1897, and the Reverend Benedict M. Rajcany, who had been ordained a priest five years earlier in Hungary, was placed in charge. The present cathedral, shown here, was finished in 1930.
Photo by Allan.

Faiths For All Seasons

Lake County is so thickly populated with churches that, through them, it is possible to trace the development of western religion.

Most residents are Roman Catholic, Greek Orthodox (including Serbian, Macedonian, etc.), Greek Catholic, Episcopalian, Polish Independent, Romanian Independent, Protestant, and Jewish. Their melange of holy houses directly or indirectly descend from the ancient Jewish church and reflect the country of origin of many Lake County people.

Christians organized churches in most of the cities of the Roman Empire, where clergy usually conducted services in the speech of the city—Latin in western Europe, other languages elsewhere. Although Latin evolved into Spanish, French, Italian, and Romanian, priests in western Europe continued to use Latin. But in eastern Europe, priests conducted services in the vernacular, and the form of the services also differed.

After Temple Beth'el held its first service in 1907 to serve the thirty-six Jewish families in Gary, Temple Israel, a Reformed congregation, followed in 1910. Gary August, a famed scholar and man of cultured tastes, served the latter as a rabbi from 1926 to 1951. The synagogue relocated to Miller Beach in 1959. Here is a baby-naming ceremony at Temple Israel. PhotoCalumet image by Karen Callaway.

In 1054, European Christians split, one group acknowledging the leadership of the Pope in Rome, the other acknowledging the leadership of the Patriarch of Constantinople. Those in western Europe became known as Roman Catholics, those in eastern Europe as Greek Orthodox. A third group in central Europe acknowledged the Pope but conducted services in the vernacular in a form similar to the Greek Orthodox church; these people were called Greek Catholics. A fourth group was made up of congregations that remained independent of either group. Since Lake County drew most of its population from all over Europe and Asia Minor, all four of these groups of churches are represented in the county.

The Whiting Baptist Church, shown here, looks like it belongs in a New England countryside, instead of just a few feet away from what was once the world's largest complete refinery, Standard Oil of Indiana. Photo by Ed Rudzinski.

Gertrude and Vincent Ortega pray after a priest of St. Joseph's (Hammond) placed ashes on their fore- heads at the start of Lent. Times photo by Geoffrey Black.

The Methodists in Lake County first conducted services in Hammond in 1872, although no church was formally established until 1881. Here is the Woodmar United Methodist Church, one of many churches that migrated to suburban neigh- borhoods following World War II. Photo by Gene Korba for Carle Communications.

On Good Friday, many Catholics in East Chicago and Indiana Harbor re-enact "the way of the cross," complete with the type of raiment worn two thousand years ago, and a cross of the type on which Jesus Christ was crucified. PhotoCalumet image by Karen Callaway.

Bishop Dale Melczek, Gary Diocese, sprinkles holy water over the altar during a Mass celebrating the renovation of Holy Angels Cathedral, which he called "the majestic mother church." Times photo by Tracy Albano.

Many religious rites are administered in Lake County churches, including the practice of healing and anointing, as seen here at the First Church of God. PhotoCalumet image by Karen Callaway.

"The Church of all Nations" is the name given the First Baptist Church of Indiana Harbor. Each Sunday, two services are given at the church, one in English and one in Spanish. Photo by Patricia Young McKinlay.

Homes For All Purses

Before one's very eyes, the appearance of housing in Lake County changes, like an unfolding flower. Where there were fields there are now communities; where there were marginal houses and buildings there are now rejuvenated homes. And while it is impossible to say when it will all end, there's little question as to when it started. During the budget-conscious recession years of the 1970s and early 1980s, wave after wave of newcomers from Illinois washed over the state line to become Lake County Hoosiers.

This set off a housing boom in Lake County where a buyer could find a diverse and plentiful housing mix at prices well below comparable homes in the immediate Chicago area. These Lake County homes were, and are, complemented by first-rate schools, exceptional recreational outlets, opportunities for rich cultural and arts experiences, and other amenities of the good life.

The transformed quality of life in Lake County has since been recognized by *Money* magazine, whose prestigious "Best Places to Live" department ranks Northwest Indiana sixtieth in the nation. In the process of achieving that rating, the megalopolis of Northwest Indiana has passed such cities as Chicago, Indianapolis, and Milwaukee.

Typically, a home selling for $200,000 in a Chicago suburb can be bought for $150,000 in Lake County, with property tax rates often twenty-five percent lower than those in Illinois.
Photo courtesy of Carle Communications.

Facing page: Movement toward neo-traditional housing developments, similar to Marktown in Indiana Harbor (shown here), is beginning to find expression in Lake County. These modern-day villages are created with pedestrian-friendly streets and a mix of housing types ranging from townhome to large upscale homes all within a few blocks of each other. Art by Mitch Markovitz.

Season's Greetings

From Marktown, Indiana Harbor and all your Family and Friends in Northwest Indiana... Just around the corner along the

South Shore Line

Boys find places to exhaust their energies, even in sturdy neighborhoods. Here Luke Reubelt, 17, and Shawn Johnson, 15 (rear), practice their art in the Johnsons' backyard. Times *photo by Zbigniew Bzdak.*

Lake County's housing stock includes many structures of historic significance, such as this one built by Andrew Wickey in East Chicago more than a century ago. Photo by Patricia Young McKinlay.

Truly unique living is achieved by a lucky few, like Gene and Judy Ayers, whose home in Miller Beach abuts Lake Michigan. A short stroll down a sandy trail leads to the beach. Photo by Patricia Young McKinlay.

Left: Large, sturdy, handsome homes exist in a number of neighborhoods in Lake County. Here is a street in Whiting that exhibits such homes. Photo by Patricia Young McKinlay.

Above: Scattered about Lake County are many estates, large homes sitting on at least an acre of land and usually a good deal more. *Times* photo by Aldino Gallo.

Little by little Lake County land is being scarfed up for new houses and housing developments. Mark Humpfer of Stump Busters, shown here, inspects the brush of an Eagle Ridge lot in Schererville. *Times* photo by Tracy Albano.

World-Class Shopping

While many residents of Lake County make short, special shopping trips into Chicago's loop and North Michigan Avenue, many more stay at home and take advantage of the incredible diversity of stores and shops within a few minutes' driving time.

In Crown Point, the Old Lake County Courthouse has become the voguish place to shop for an unusual gift, while getting a good whiff of Lake County history. Photo courtesy of Edda Taylor Photographic.

Indeed, the intersection of U.S. 30 and Interstate 65 in Merrillville and Hobart is a modern bazaar of shops, not to mention being an entertainment mecca.

From bookstores to the great outdoors, from quaint boutiques to large malls, Lake County has shops and shopping for everyone. Many of these shops are found in Southlake Mall, a regional shopping center in Hobart with a hundred stores, including four anchors, all under one roof. The mall is a magnet that attracts customers from a seventy-five-mile radius. Just across U.S. 30 from Southlake is Crossroads Shopping Plaza featuring a variety of specialty stores and restaurants. And just down the road to the west in Merrillville is Century Mall, which offers even more outstanding shopping and dining opportunities. All are within minutes of one another.

Other mall opportunities include Woodmar Mall in Hammond and the Village Shopping Center in Gary, as well as sparkling new shopping plazas in Highland and Schererville. Apart from these marketing colossuses, dozens of strip malls serve neighborhood needs as do traditional downtowns that exist in Griffith, Hobart, Whiting, Highland, Indiana Harbor, Miller Beach, and other communities.

The vicinity of the intersection of Interstate 65 and U.S. 30 contains more stores than the downtowns of many major cities. Southlake Mall comprises mega-stores like L.S. Ayres of Indianapolis and Kohl's, as well as dozens of specialty shops, such as The Disney Store, Kaybee Toys, and Talbots. Other diversity of style can be found at nearby Crossroads Shopping Plaza and Century Mall, which features a number of off-price stores. *Times* photo by Aldino Gallo.

Custom Imports is one of a number of specialty stores that can be found on the recently rebuilt Lake Street in Miller Beach. Photo by Patricia Young McKinlay.

Old-fashioned downtowns, where people walk the entire length of the main street buying their necessities and luxuries and gossiping with neighbors, can be found in several Lake County communities. They are typified by 119th Street in Whiting, shown here. Photo by Allan.

Top: First of Lake County's suburban shopping centers, Woodmar Mall in Hammond was built in the mid-1950s, enclosed in the 1980s, and continues as one of the most pleasant shopping venues in Lake County. Carson Pirie Scott anchors the mall, which contains a variety of stores usually found in a regional mall. Photo by Richard D. Rudzinski.

Fresh produce abounds in Lake County, where people whose ancestors often came from the growing fields of far-off lands have a special appreciation for high-quality vegetables and fruits. Here a woman shops at the Delray market, which specializes in produce that appeals to certain ethnic groups. Times photo by Zbigniew Bzdak.

Wellness Is Big Business

For a variety of reasons, healthcare has become one of the most important industries in Lake County. In fact, hospitals have become the largest employers in some of the county's once industry-dominated cities. A diverse assortment, the hospitals are the workshops of physicians who not only conduct general practices but offer a wide range of specialties. Even some Illinois residents choose to cross the state line and have their healthcare needs met in Lake County, not only because of the high quality of care offered, but because Lake County's costs tend to be below the national average.

St. Margaret Mercy Hospitals and Health Care Centers, a general hospital in Hammond and Dyer, also specializes in behavioral medicine, women's services, pain management, rehabilitation, and home care. The Hammond unit, shown here, also excels in cardiovascular services and operates an oncology center, and the only pediatric intensive-care unit in Northwest Indiana. Photo courtesy of Carle Communications.

Community Hospital of Munster operates the county's largest cardiac program, its heart center being a partnership between physicians and the hospital. Photo by Richard D. Rudzinski.

Facing page: Tradewinds Rehabilitation Center in Gary has, in its various manifestations, been serving Lake County for more than a half century. Its mission is to enhance the lives of children and adults with disabilities and special challenges by producing goods and services that contribute to the quality of life and economic well-being of the community. Art by John Rush.

INDEPENDENCE

TradeWinds Affirmative Industries

It's Just Around the Corner Along the

SOUTH SHORE LINE

chapter 3

Another Day, Another Dollar

"If you can't make a buck in Lake County, you can't make a nickel anywhere else," was a saying that rippled through America for many years. Another one common among immigrants went further: "Even dead men get hired in Gary."

Neither of those sayings would apply today when, regardless of the task, occupational emphasis is on education, training, and skills, skills, skills. While other places may theorize about technology, Lake County applies it to every cranny of a traditional mill, and depends on it completely in businesses that exist largely in cyberspace. Unlike the "old days" when a strong back was the main requisite for mill employment, today's workers in Lake County are finely trained for the challenges of the new millennium.

Big Shoulders

Steel remains king in Lake County, mainly because the three major producers—LTV, Ispat Inland, and U.S. Steel—have infused hundreds of millions of dollars into computerized, state-of-the-art operations, increasing output while improving efficiency and reducing pollution.

Based on building the first truly refrigerated railroad car, George H. Hammond, Marcus M. Towle, Caleb Ives, and George W. Plumer formed a partnership to build, in 1869, the State Line Slaughter-House in Hammond. Drawing courtesy of the Calumet Room of Hammond's main library.

Today, Lake County and neighboring Porter County produce about a quarter of the nation's steel, easily surpassing other well-known steel regions. Although employment shrank considerably during the efficiency-driven nineties, output expanded, and some thirty thousand people in the two counties still make their living producing steel.

And here's the paradox: while heavy industry in Lake County has been downsized, it keeps growing.

work

Much of Ispat Inland Steel's Indiana Harbor Works is on a man-made peninsula that extends about three miles into Lake Michigan. Ispat Inland Steel photo.

Strange beauty unfolds whenever an industrial plant leans against twilight. Photo by Tom Hocker.

Facing page: Strength and Beauty Poster. Art by John Rush.

STRENGTH AND BEAUTY

THRIVE SIDE BY SIDE IN THE NATION'S PREMIERE STEELMAKING REGION ON LAKE MICHIGAN'S SOUTHERN SHORE. DRAWN BY THE WATER, WILDLIFE AND INDUSTRY SHARE THIS PLACE OF RARE DIVERSITY... *JUST AROUND THE CORNER...*

along the SOUTH SHORE LINE

The Indiana Harbor Ship Canal, once known as the inner harbor, was built in 1901 as a condition of Inland Steel's building a million dollar open hearth plant on Lake Michigan. The canal cuts a mile-and-a-half inland, with steel mills on both sides, then forks in two directions: one fork runs directly south to a connection with the Grand Calumet River, the other directly west to a connection with Lake George. When Jones & Laughlin built a steel plant in Hammond, the immediate connection with Lake George was filled in with cinders from Inland Steel, although most of the Lake George Branch continued to provide docks for Standard Oil, Sinclair, and Socony Vacuum oil refineries. Times photo by Zbigniew Bzdak.

Steel mills seem at times to be almost alive, huffing and puffing, clamorous, intimidating, yet with a fascination that is unique among workplaces. Photo by Tom Hocker.

Today's skilled workers spend much of their time in control rooms, like this one, routinely applying technical knowledge that would have given their untrained forebears cluster headaches. Photo by Tom Hocker.

A person entering a modern steel mill could be excused for thinking he was Gulliver in the land of Brobdingnagians. Compare the worker, lower right, with this slab crane. LTV Steel photo.

Above: Here, in this sinter plant, a bonded mass of metal particles is shaped and partially fused by pressure and heat below the melting point. LTV Steel photo.

Right: A stop like this one before a basic oxygen furnace is one of several on an LTV tour. LTV Steel photo.

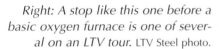

Above: Among the finished products of a steel mill are those that are flat-rolled, coated, and coiled. LTV Steel photo.

Left: Some idea of the complexity of today's steel-making can be gleaned from this view of a six-stand tandem mill in LTV's Tin Mill. LTV Steel photo.

The Lighter Side

The transition from the Industrial Age to the Information Age induced an outbreak of entrepreneurialship in Lake County, and new businesses created new jobs.

During the heyday of the Industrial Age, producers of primary products in Lake County spawned hundreds of secondary industries, such as steel fabricators and various users of petroleum and its by-products. With the downsizing of primary product producers, many of its ancillary industries have dried up and blown away. Some have not, though, especially those that applied a healthy dose of modern technology to their businesses. Ogden Engineering Corporation in Schererville, for example, supplies automated welding systems for almost every structural steel and shipbuilding company in the United States and the world.

Some new businesses have been spawned by changes in laws. With utility companies free to wholesale megawatts of electricity to each other, what became Arc Information Technologies (Arc IT)

Champion Corporation began more than a century ago when Otto Knoezer, a blacksmith, invented an automatic potato digger. Today's products are more exotic. Here, Bob Houser of St. John works on a part for an underground cable puller. *Times* photo by Zbigniew Bzdak.

seized the opportunity. In 1996, the Lake County company developed a computer application to help utility traders track all information needed to buy and sell electricity efficiently. Since then, electricity trading has become an expanding industry, growing at 400 percent per year, and expected to be a $4.5 trillion business by the year 2002.

Taking advantage of new technology, Don Burrell, with a partner, began to process color photographs in 1959, two years after Kodak introduced color processing. Today, Burrell owns ten processing labs in Florida, Montana, and California, and Burrell Professional Labs now forms the largest network of labs catering to professional photographers. Each November and December alone, Burrell's main plant in Crown Point processes a thousand orders a day from professional portrait studios across the nation.

Nick Floyd (foreground) and LeRoy Howard started a new micro-brewery, called Three Floyds, in an old building on Calumet Avenue in Hammond. Times *photo by Tracy Albano.*

Traditional peasant girls in long skirts are sometimes replaced at Lake Michigan Winery in Robertsdale by young men of great endurance, preferably marathon runners. Stomping at the winery takes place twice a year. Photo courtesy of Lake Michigan Winery.

Land of Milk and Honey

Until 1869, farming was not only the biggest industry in Lake County but virtually the only one. Even when heavy industry captured the extreme north of the county, farming continued to be an important economic wellspring. With exurbanization, however, the major crops of many farms today are split-levels, ranches, and townhouses.

Nevertheless, many farms remain in Lake County and are more productive than ever. And, of course, the original farms are the basis for everything that came after them. To celebrate Lake County's heritage as a major farming center, the county has preserved Buckley Homestead, a 1910 working farm, for younger generations to see how it was in the olden days. Buckley is one of eleven Lake County Parks.

Modern Lake County farmers use modern tools, and in the case of Richard and Geraldine Wunderlink of Lowell that includes a small airplane. St. Petersburg *Times* photo.

To reduce their vulnerability to the elements, Lake County farmers employ equipment that was not available to their predecessors. Here a coil of irrigation equipment has been positioned to water a farm in Hobart. Photo by Patricia Young McKinlay.

One of the important facets of Lake County agriculture today is the output of greenhouses, some of which can be found in Dyer along Route 30. Times photo by John J. Watkins.

GOBBLE FRESH

In Eagle Creek Township near Hebron, people line up to pick a freshly-slaughtered turkey at the Morrow Turkey Farm. These are turkeys for connoisseurs who would have no turkey other than a fresh one.

For more than eight decades, these fresh turkey fanciers have trekked to Morrow's, and a constituency of many others has joined them. The buyers reverted to fresh turkeys because they believe the birds are moister and juicier than frozen turkeys, and have an even more distinct aroma when prepared. Morrow's turkeys are also said to be easier to work with because they're fresh and soft, instead of thawed and tough.

The Morrows got their start in turkeys right after World War I when Johanna's husband, Neil, then 10, began selling turkeys as a way to make extra spending money. Neil died at age 86 in 1993, but his widow and seven children continued the tradition he began. As in the past, a person in Lake County who wants to "talk turkey" finds a receptive audience at Morrow's.

There is reason to believe that Johnny Appleseed visited Lake County and that he left behind the apple trees whose descendants yield a bountiful crop. Here, a young girl shows how it's done during an apple fest near Deep River County Park. Times photo by Aldino Gallo.

Don Ewen represents the new wave of educated farmers in that he is a product of Valparaiso University. Photo by Patricia Young McKinlay.

A Day Away

Centrally located, Lake County sits within a day's drive of most Americans and Canadians. Put another way, two-thirds of the U.S. and Canadian populations fall within a six-hundred-mile radius of Lake County, all of whom can reach Lake County within a day. Thus, Lake County has become a popular destination for people wishing to have a good time, and is an air, rail, water, and highway hub for not only domestic but international trade and commerce.

Persons landing at all Chicago airports—O'Hare International, Midway, and Meigs—can easily and quickly access Lake County, which is home to a fourth Chicago area airport: the Gary/Chicago Airport which is serviced by Pan American Airlines. Gary/Chicago has the second-longest runway in Greater Chicago, and has become an important facility for private aircraft that swoop in for quickie visits to casinos and/or one of the county's refreshing recreational spots. Including air freight, the airport handles more than sixty thousand flights a year. Gary/Chicago also contains an eighty-four-hundred-acre Airport Development Zone, which provides tax advantages to new industries. Indeed the potential of the airport has scarcely been scratched.

Because of its importance in the Chicago aviation system, Gary/Chicago has become a partner in a joint bi-state airport authority, and has already received from Chicago more than a million dollars for capital improvements. The authority was formed in 1995 to oversee development at Gary/Chicago in addition to O'Hare and Midway.

Overland, four major interstates cut through Lake County— I-65, I-80, I-90, and I-94—offering routes from both coasts, the Gulf of Mexico, and Canada. Other Midwest and Southern locations connect with Lake County via I-55 and I-57, whose primary destination is nearby Chicago. These connections, combined with its central location, make Lake County

Lake County could hardly be more centrally located. Within one day's drive, or 600 miles, one can find two-thirds of the population of the United States and Canada. Those traveling by train are serviced by several Amtrak stations; those flying usually shuttle from/to Chicago O'Hare or Midway; and those who fly in private jets land at convenient Gary/Chicago Airport, less than 15 minutes from three Lake Michigan casinos. Map courtesy of the Lake County Convention and Visitors Bureau.

Approximate distance from Lake County to these major cities in the Midwest:	
Chicago, IL	20 mi.
St. Louis, MO	300 mi.
Indianapolis, IN	120 mi.
Detroit, MI	230 mi.
South Bend, IN	50 mi.
Milwaukee, WI	125 mi.
Louisville, KY	225 mi.
Fort Wayne, IN	120 mi.
Columbus, OH	275 mi.
Cleveland, OH	300 mi.

LAKE COUNTY
INDIANA
CONVENTION & VISITORS BUREAU

Gary/Chicago Airport.

attractive to visitors and to many different types of industries. For example, Lake County is in the middle of the continent's largest auto-producing areas: Michigan, Ohio, Illinois, and Ontario. Moreover, the enormous Chicago market is actually more accessible from Lake County than from many parts of Northeast Illinois.

Rail links connect the Chicago rail hub to Lake County, eight carriers serving Lake County, in addition to twenty-five carriers being available in the Chicago rail yards. Intermodal operations are located a few miles away in Remington, where Toledo Peoria & Western operates a terminal. Burlington Northern provides direct intermodal access to the western states.

The South Shore Line rail passenger service is another important railway asset, with an annual ridership of about 3.5 million passengers. The last interurban electric line in the nation, the South Shore speeds passengers to and from downtown Chicago in less than a hour. Some fifty-five hundred Indiana residents commute to work in Chicago on the South Shore Line, and many Chicago area residents use the South Shore to reach recreational locations along the shore of Lake Michigan. The South Shore Freight Railroad also runs on the same track and operates as an independent regional carrier.

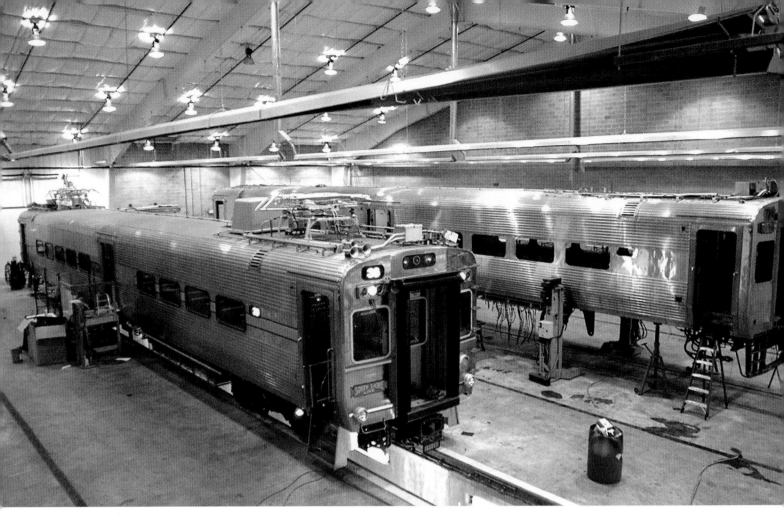

The South Shore Line is the country's last electrified interurban rail line. Annual ridership of 3.5 million continues to grow. Cars are seen here being serviced at "The Shops," in Michigan City. *Times* photo by Sam Riche.

The Cline Avenue Extension, shown here "coming in for a landing" in Indiana Harbor, is the most expensive stretch of highway in Indiana. *Times* photo by Geoffrey Black.

*For most of the twenti-
eth century, the
Indiana Harbor Ship
Canal was Indiana's
largest and busiest
port. By 1930, more
ships from foreign
countries docked at
Indiana Harbor than
any other port on
lower Lake Michigan.
At the same time,
Indiana Harbor
shipped more gasoline
than any other port in
America.* Photo by
Richard D. Rudzinski.

*The striking Gary Public Transportation Center coordinates a variety of travel modes,
including the South Shore Railroad and city buses.* Photo by Richard D. Rudzinski.

Railroads enter Lake County from all directions, exemplified by the crossing shown here. Photo by Paul A. Meyers.

The Times, *selected Indiana's best
daily newspaper five times in the 1990s,
occupies a relatively new building in Munster, shown here,
which is a study in cyberspace.* Photo by Patricia Young McKinlay.

Above: The Gary/Chicago Airport is used for both commercial and industrial purposes, but is also home to the "Confederate Airforce," a group of aviation devotees who spend their weekends flying old airplanes. Photo by Richard D. Rudzinski.

While Lake County residents receive much of their radio and TV fare from Chicago stations, the county does have a public broadcasting TV station, WYIN, Channel 56, and several TCI cable studios. It also has a variety of radio stations. Shown here is the transmitting tower of WJOB in Woodmar (Hammond). Photo by Richard D. Rudzinski.

chapter 4

Recreation in All Forms

Thanks to the beneficence of a retreating glacier as the Ice Age took a curtain call, and to the foresight of more recent county leaders, Lake County is blessed with more recreational opportunities than an expensive resort. From the majestic sand dunes near Lake Michigan to the marshes of the Kankakee River, opportunities for inexpensive recreation abound, limited only by one's energy, ambition, and imagination.

The beaches of north county provide all manner of fun, exercise, and rejuvenation, while, throughout the county, one of the premier park systems in the nation features unmatched fun, flora, and fauna. Nature is the catalyst. For the outdoorsman and birder, all varieties of waterfowl and other feathery creatures abound along the Lake Michigan flyways, which funnel into Lake County from Lake Michigan and continue southward to the Kankakee. For the hunter, whitetail deer roam abundantly in the southern forests and farmlands.

Lake County is also home to what's left of the Grand Kankakee Marsh, a natural stopover for hundreds of thousands of migrating ducks and geese each fall. Nuzzling the banks of the Kankakee River, the residual marsh contains a county park with public hunting and photography blinds, as well as a public boat launch. For the angler, Lake County offers many fishing opportunities, not only in The Big Lake but in a number of inland lakes, streams, and rivers. In fact, Lake County is the proud home of more state fishing records than any other county in Indiana.

Lake County beaches have long been a favorite setting of photographers shooting fashion pictures. Here, pin-up girl Lorraine Brokskar (Otto) models an informal fashion that was popular during the post–World War II period. Photo by Russ Moore.

play

Swimming

Lake County beaches stretch from the Illinois-Indiana state line to the Lake-Porter county line, interrupted from time to time by heavy industry. The beach then extends into Porter County, where industry also occasionally intrudes itself, and then into LaPorte County and on up into Michigan. Much of the extended beach is among the finest in the world, and its singing (squeaky) sands are unique.

Going eastward from the stateline, the first beach is Hammond's Lake Front Beach and Bird Sanctuary, which ends at the Hammond Marina. Next comes Whiting's Whihala Beach, which is also a county park. The next to the east is Jeorse Park in Indiana Harbor, hard by Buffington Pier, which is the smallest of the beaches and a remnant of B.A.B., once famous as the haunt of skinny dippers. A few miles to the east is Pine Beach at the foot of Clark Road in Gary, now largely abandoned. The next three public beaches are all in Miller (Gary): Lake Street Beach at the foot of Lake Street, Marquette Park Beach, and Wells Street Beach.

Swimming at these beaches, naturally, is the big attraction, followed closely by bathers who just want to get wet and cool off. Between swims, people lounge on the beach soaking up the sun, although carefully, given the present-day respect for the sun's ability to injure the skin as well as tan it. The loungers also become spectators of a sort of non-stop fashion show, during which the comeliest of young women and the hunkiest of young men promenade along the shoreline for the edification of all manner of critics. It is a tradition as old as the nineteenth amendment to the U.S. Constitution.

Perhaps the most popular of the South Shore posters produced in the 1920s was the "Girl on the Beach," which has been reproduced many times over the years and has become a collectors' item. As part of a new Millennium Series of South Shore posters, the Northwest Indiana Forum has updated the "Girl," shown here. Art by Fred Semmler.

One of the most popular water attractions in Lake County is still the traditional swimming pool, which can be found in several city parks. Here, classes are being held in lifesaving at the Hub Pool in Crown Point, which has been a popular attraction for more than thirty years. *Times* photo by John J. Watkins.

Coexistence of nature and industry is a uniqueness of Lake County that drives hard-core environmentalists to distraction. Nevertheless, coexistence thrives, seen here as two picnicking young women promenade on the beach with a steel mill in the background. *Times* photo by Tracy Albano.

Boating

The forty-five miles of Lake Michigan shoreline in Lake County are not just beaches and industry. Large, new marinas have sprung up in Hammond and Indiana Harbor, and more are in the talking stage. Lake County has some two thousand slips and counting. The two most highly-regarded marinas are the Robert A. Pastrick Marina in Indiana Harbor, with its two hundred fifty slips, outstanding boat storage facilities, and forty acres of parkland; and the Hammond Marina, one of the nation's largest, which contains one thousand one hundred thirteen slips, five launch ramps, and fishing piers.

In addition to these Lake Michigan marinas, a great many boats are docked at inland Cedar Lake, where the annual regatta is a major event and where weekly races occupy the entire summer. The three largest of the mooring places are the Cedar Lake Boat Launch, La Tulip's Harbor, and Pine Crest Marina.

Hybrid vehicles have become enormously popular along the south Lake Michigan Coast. Headquarters for most of them is Wells Street Beach in Miller. Photo by Marilyn Parker.

Wind surfing thrives at Wolf Lake because it is a natural wind alley. This has made Wolf Lake the premier surf sailing venue in Greater Chicago, if not the Midwest. Times photo by Tracy Albano.

Sailing on The Big Lake bears some relationship to sailing on an ocean, so it is not a sport for the untrained. Here, Skipper Jeff Barrow, a Lake Michigan instructor, adjusts the main sail after a sudden shift in the wind.
Times photo by Tracy Albano.

The canoe, while not as commonplace as when the Potawatomi occupied the land, has made a major comeback in Lake County, both as a recreation vehicle and as a practical mode of transportation. Here, members of the Grand Calumet River Task Force use canoes to carry out their mission of promoting the health of the river. Photo courtesy of the Grand Calumet Task Force.

Above: The Robert A. Pastrick Marina in Indiana Harbor, shown here, boasts two hundred fifty slips and forty acres of parkland. Photo courtesy of East Chicago Room.

The Hammond Marina in Robertsdale, shown here, is one of the nation's largest, containing 1,113 slips, five launch ramps, and fishing piers. Photo courtesy of the Lake County Convention and Visitors Bureau.

Hooked on Fishing

The quantity of fish pulled out of The Big Lake was once measured not in inches but in tons. For a variety of reasons, not the least of which is the invasion of fish released from the ballast tanks of foreign ships, native fish no longer always grow to maturity. That's because these gauche invaders nosh on critical parts of the food chain. Thus, Lake Michigan is not the piscatorial cornucopia it was more than a century ago when Bob Carr and other professionals at Miller Beach caught fish in nets so heavy they had to be pulled out of the water by means of windlasses on the beach. Nor is it the same as in 1905 when Albert Sabinske caught an eight-foot sturgeon that weighed more than two hundred pounds. Nor is it the same as just a few years ago when perch practically jumped into fishers' boats. But Lake Michigan, and inland lakes, still has plenty of fish, the catching of which attracts the true fisherman. Indeed, many compete in contests, such as annual coho salmon tournaments.

Because of various anti-pollution laws and the purifying nature of such otherwise nuisance foreign fish as zebra mussels, Lake Michigan is cleaner than at any time in the past century. In fact, chinook salmon are so impressed with the quality of the water leaving the East Chicago wastewater treatment plant that they swim five miles from Lake Michigan to lay eggs in the plant's contact chambers. Freshwater sponges also have taken up residence there.

Fishing is a universal endeavor in Lake County, where anglers begin at a young age, as is the case here, and continue into their twilight years. Times *photo by John Watkins.*

Marquette Trail, which parallels Long Lake in Miller Beach and across the county line, leads to West Beach, an increasingly popular swimming hole.
Photo courtesy of Indiana Dunes National Lakeshore.

Anglers bragging about the best fishing hole in Lake County could go on all day because there are so many choices. But there is one verity. The bait and equipment trade is a brisk one. *Times* photo by Trace Albano.

Golf

When recreationists are not desporting themselves in Lake Michigan and other public basins of Lake County, they can often be found on the golf course. In all, Lake County has twenty top-notch public courses, in addition to a number of well-groomed country clubs. The most heavily-used of the courses is in Wicker Park, a township facility comprising several hundred acres of wooded recreation, including picnic grounds, sand volleyball courts, and other facilities to help people revive themselves in their leisure.

Lake County courses are wide-ranging, in that a person can find one to suit his talents, from hacker to seasoned pro. Most of the courses also offer full-service banquet facilities, pro shops, meeting rooms, and a nineteenth-hole. Besides the courses contained in Lake County, golfers can easily reach a total of forty courses within an hour's drive. Residents of Lake County have within easy driving distance of their homes more than two hundred fifty parks and dozens of freshwater lakes and streams.

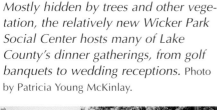

Mostly hidden by trees and other vegetation, the relatively new Wicker Park Social Center hosts many of Lake County's dinner gatherings, from golf banquets to wedding receptions. Photo by Patricia Young McKinlay.

Below: Beautiful Woodmar Country Club, a one hundred-ten-acre, eighteen-hole paradise in Saxony (Hammond) was part of an ambitious six hundred forty-acre real estate development. It was started in 1923 by ex-Times reporter Roscoe Woods and future Hammond mayor Frank Martin (Wood + Mar = Woodmar), following Hammond's 1923 annexation of Hessville, which had swallowed Saxony in 1917. Photo courtesy of Carle Communications.

Left: The eighteen-hole golf course at Wicker Park is part of Lake County's largest recreational center. Photo by Patricia Young McKinlay.

Above: Once the sport of the well-to-do, golf in Lake County now has an egalitarian quality to it, as people of all incomes enjoy the county's many courses. Photo courtesy of the Lake County Visitors and Convention Bureau.

Left: U.S. Steel Supervisors' Club operates a golf course and recently built the beautiful structure shown here. The course can now be played by the general public. Photo by Patricia Young McKinlay.

Dunes

Lake Michigan defines Lake County, in more ways than one. The lake overflows with things magical and mystical, but none so much as sand, which shapes itself into lush dunes and ridges and

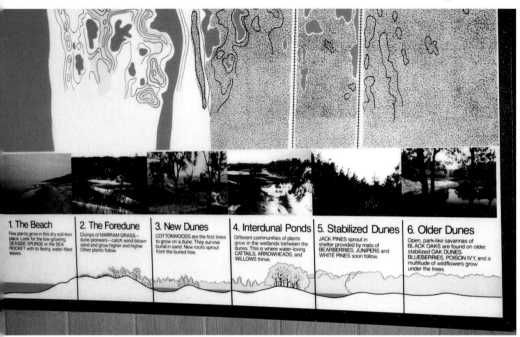

1. The Beach	2. The Foredune	3. New Dunes	4. Interdunal Ponds	5. Stabilized Dunes	6. Older Dunes
Few plants grow in this dry soil-less place. Look for the low-growing SEASIDE SPURGE or the SEA ROCKET with its fleshy, water-filled leaves.	Clumps of MARRAM GRASS—dune pioneers—catch wind-blown sand and grow higher and higher. Other plants follow.	COTTONWOODS are the first trees to grow on a dune. They survive burial in sand. New roots sprout from the buried tree.	Different communities of plants grow in the wetlands between the dunes. This is where water-loving CATTAILS, ARROWHEADS, and WILLOWS thrive.	JACK PINES sprout in shelter provided by mats of BEARBERRIES, JUNIPERS and WHITE PINES soon follow.	Open, park-like savannas of BLACK OAKS are found on older, stabilized OAK DUNES. BLUEBERRIES, POISON IVY, and a multitude of wildflowers grow under the trees.

A dunes succession exhibit, shown here, is just one facet of the Paul H. Douglas Center for Environmental Education, located at Miller Woods. A 7,000-square-foot structure, the Center includes space for audio-visual, offices, assembly rooms, and a partial basement. Outside, it provides board-walks (through the woods), a forty vehicle parking lot, five hundred feet of roadway, and a vehicle storage building. Through the Douglas Center, tens of thousands of school children learn about the environment, as they gain an understanding and appreciation of their unique surroundings.
Photo by Patricia Young McKinlay.

other captivating forms. Fascinated people from all over the world rate the Indiana dunes an attraction comparable to the most celebrated national parks. Indeed, the Indiana Dunes National Lakeshore, part of which is in Lake County, attracts some two million visitors a year.

Today, Miller Beach (Gary) is the gateway to the dune country. It is the beginning of dune ridges that rise at points east of Lake County to almost two hundred feet above Lake Michigan. Within these dunes lie interdunal ponds and blowouts that extend a mile or so inland. Behind the dunes lies the Great Marsh, a band of swampy terrain extending from Lake Street in Miller Beach across Porter County to Michigan City in LaPorte County. A bit to the south, another band of dunes provide the foundation for the Chicago, South Bend, and South Shore Railroad (The South Shore), as well as a series of highways and roads. Still another low ridge of dunes abuts the wetlands of the Grand and Little Calumet Rivers.

In addition to many recreational opportunities, the dunes have been the scene of scientific progress. Just before the turn of the century, Henry Chandler Cowles made the dunes the birthplace of ecology. He established the dunes as a classic landscape for the study of ecological succession. A simplification of his concept can be viewed at the Douglas Environmental Center at Miller Woods.

Not only did the dunes give birth to ecology but to manned flight. In 1896, French-born Octave Chanute, a famous bridge designer, built a variety of gliders that he tested from a high dune in Miller and at points to the east. The body design of his best glider became the model for the fuselage of the Wright Brothers' Kitty Hawk plane. The complete story on Chanute can be found at the Acquatorium on the beach of Marquette Park in Miller.

Miller Woods, which features open oak savannah and interdunal ponds together with pines and cottonwoods, exemplifies stages in dunes succession. Its trails run from one to three miles. Photo courtesy of Indiana Dunes National Lakeshore.

When Wilbur and Orville Wright took the first flight in a self-propelled heavier-than-air craft in 1903, they credited for the body Octave Chanute, a famous railroad

bridge builder. Seven years earlier, Chanute had conducted breakthrough glider experiments on the dunes of Miller Beach and dunes to the east. Wilbur, an Indiana native, wrote that Chanute "had vast influence in bringing about the era of human flight." Photo courtesy of the Calumet Regional Archives of Indiana University Northwest.

Nature

Lake County contains some of the most inspiring natural scenery in Indiana. High on the list are the dunes, which lure people from all over the world and which begin in Lake County. Part of the Indiana Dunes National Lakeshore is in Lake County and, via Marquette Trail next to Long Lake, blends into the West Beach area of Porter County. In this territory swimming, biking, hiking, camping, and cross-country skiing are just a few of the favorite pastimes.

Miller Woods is a magical place, where sunbeams leap across the shade of a forest floor to brighten already brilliant wild flowers, and bounce over the ups and downs of the terrain, which once were naked dunes at the border of Lake Michigan. Still on the move, the sunbeams ramble along, overtaking ducks and geese and other fowl cruising about in sunken ponds, and, on a lucky day, they will land on a blue heron working a good fishing hole before flapping itself aloft.

And Miller Woods are often full of children, fresh from their lessons at the Douglas Environmental Center, which attempts to connect kids to nature. Sometimes a child will spot a deer on a hurst nearby, the first the child has seen, and the thrill of the sighting practically sets the leaves aquiver.

"Birthplace of Ecology" was the name given Lake County and the Indiana duneland when University of Chicago Professor Henry Chandler Cowles, shown here, became America's first professional ecologist. Using the dunes as his model and laboratory, Cowles theorized about the dynamics of ecological succession, which was later applied to other fields. For twenty years, starting in 1896, Cowles had visited and studied almost all of the dunes on all continents and concluded that the Lake Michigan dunes were "the grandest in the entire world." Photo courtesy of the Calumet Regional Archives of Indiana University Northwest.

Hoosier Prairie in Griffith is a flower-filled part of the Indiana Dunes National Lakeshore. It is three hundred thirty-five acres of virgin land that represents the way Indiana was before progress. The largest chunk of virgin prairie left in Indiana, Hoosier Prairie shelters more than three hundred native plants, many now rare in Indiana, which thrive here because of varying moisture conditions. Art by Alice Phillips.

Among the unusual flowers that can be found in Lake County is the prairie coneflower, shown here. Photo by Larry A. Brechner.

When pioneers settled Lake County during the first half of the nineteenth century, they rarely failed to comment on the profusion of wild flowers that caused the prairies and woods to fairly sparkle. These flowers still exist and are the object of hikes at different seasons of the year. Photo by Larry A. Brechner.

In some places, butterflies, like the one shown above, have become endangered species. Not in Griffith's Oak Ridge Prairie, where butterflies of all descriptions can be found in great profusion. Photo by Larry A. Brechner.

Dunes begin when marram grass takes root and hangs on for dear life, regardless of pressures on it. As wind and wave send sand upon the shore, the grass restrains some of it from returning across the beach to the lake. As the sand piles up over the years and is shaped by the elements, it gradually becomes a dune and moves slowly inland. Photo courtesy of Northwest Indiana Forum.

Birding

Lake County is one of the great bird-watching vantage points in the nation. Some three hundred thirty-seven avian species have been identified and more are suspected. About one hundred thirteen are regular nesters, another twenty-four are occasional nesters, and the jury is still out on nine more.

Lake Michigan influences birdlife in Lake County more than anything else. It provides habitat for open water species; affects local migration patterns; and supports a wide beach that draws to it numerous waders. Singular pockets of habitat, plus the steadying effects of the dunes' microclimate, encourage nesting sites for such birds as passerines, which usually haunt more southern climes. Others reside just to the south of the dunes.

The Funnel Effect is caused by the cone that is Lake Michigan. The shores of The Big Lake provide leading lines that control flight paths of numerous migrants, while its vast open waters attract uncountable numbers of transitory and wintering birds. During the fall, the elongated north-south boundaries of the lake become air-

The duneland is habitat to numerous species of endangered wildlife and birds. Many are drawn to the southern shore of Lake Michigan by what is known as the Funnel Effect. Photo courtesy of the Lake County Convention and Visitors Bureau.

Lake County is one of the nation's great flyways, which attracts bird watchers from around the nation. The fall is especially popular for watching, since many birds, more associated with other climes, temporarily make their homes in Lake County, especially in the Kankakee area. A particularly good vantage point for bird watching is the parking lot at the foot of Lake Street in Miller Beach. Photo by Joanna Shearer.

3 STOOGES
FAN
PARKING
ONLY
———
N'YUK,N'YUK,N'YUK,

With its Lake Michigan coast, its mostly low-lying land, and its many inland lakes, Lake County has long been a haven for wildlife. Times photo by John J. Watkins.

ways that wintering birds by the hundreds of thousands travel. These southbound birds inevitably glide into Lake County.

This phenomenon explains why there is in Lake County each autumn an exceptionally high number of peregrine falcons, shore birds, purple sandpipers, vermillion flycatchers, and other pelagic wayfarers. More sandhill cranes congregate in Lake County and vicinity than in any other place east of the Mississippi. Most spectacular is the annual gathering of cranes: from mid-October to mid-November some sixteen thousand birds on their way from Canada to the southern United States enjoy an extended stay in the Kankakee fish and wildlife area.

A peacock seems to be an ornament on the Lake County Parks Department truck, but it's only "Mr. P." as kids visiting Buckley Homestead County Park dubbed him. Although peacocks are not uncommon in Lake County, they are mainly showy birds, used to dress up a farm or estate. Times photo by John J. Watkins.

Birds are especially thick in Lake County during the spring and fall, but can be found all year around. Once here, though, they often have to jockey for position (and food) with other birds, as these swans are doing while being harassed by seagulls at Wolf Lake. Photo by Patricia Young McKinlay.

Lake County teems with furry beasties and finny creatures, which is why sportsmen favor its many charms. But what exists today is only a suggestion of what once existed, which was called Nature's Paradise: pure streams and lakes, populated by more fish and game than any comparable region in America. Indeed, that's actually what attracted the nomadic Potawatomi to the area, especially after the fur trade began to dominate commerce on the Great Lakes.

After the settlement at Fort Dearborn evolved into Chicago, the Calumet Region of Illinois and Indiana became the "in" place for prominent Chicagoans to do their recreating. Hunting and fishing parties from Chicago usually stayed at the Eagle Hotel, about where today's 92nd Street meets Lake Michigan. From there, hired oarsmen took the guests for boat excursions through the Calumet Region. Sometimes these parties even included women, and, as an ancient author once said, "many a finny specimen was taken by the fair hand of Chicago's ladies."

When farmers arrived, they too found a great deal of wildlife, large and small. Timber wolves were everywhere, wild deer roamed in droves, lynx, foxes, woodchucks, squirrels, and weasels all abounded, and even an occasional bear was seen along the sand ridges. Raccoons in the big trees were killed for their pelts, and skunks were so plentiful that farm boys "got rich" selling their pelts for forty cents apiece. There were also more snakes along the Little Calumet and Cady Marsh (south of Munster), their breeding place, than in any other region in the nation. It was not uncommon for enterprising boys with clubs to kill five hundred large, fat snakes in a single drive through the sloughs and swamps.

chapter 5

Parks

Few counties in the nation enjoy recreational opportunities more diverse than those provided by the Lake County Parks and Recreation Department. A multi-faceted system, it comprises several thousand acres and hundreds of programs in eleven parks, each quite different from the others.

The system preserves, reclaims, and manages woodlands, wetlands, and prairies toward the goal of achieving balance in both vegetative and wildlife ecosystems. Greenways and corridors help buffer urban development and connect the county parks to a system of hiking and biking trails that link Lake County to the surrounding region. Along with these greenways, recreational opportunities increase with the addition and development of newly acquired property, geographically dispersed to provide greater access for people.

Even with eleven parks, the system continues to evolve, adapting to changing cultural, societal, and demographic demands as it seeks to meet the leisure needs of the public. The Parks Department stays alert to opportunities for acquiring, reclaiming, and preserving natural systems and open spaces, as well as expanding recreational amenities. In addition to providing more leisure opportunities, the preservation of stream and river corridors helps improve water quality and sustain watershed integrity in the face of increasing development pressure.

parks

Whihala Beach County Park

Situated on Lake Michigan, Whihala Beach County Park has been a favorite place of swimmers, boaters, and even sightseers, since the park opened on April 1, 1987. Its boat launch is open daily 4:30 a.m. to 7:00 p.m. through November, and its daily launch fee includes the parking fee for car and trailer. For frequent users, season passes are available at the gate house or the Lake County Parks business office.

Certified lifeguards supervise swimming at a beach (and beach house) that is open Memorial Day through Labor Day, from 10:00 a.m. until 7:00 p.m. The beach house concession stand is also open daily through the summer, serving pop, ice cream, and sandwiches.

Whihala is right next door to the Hammond Marina and is linked to it via bicycle and walking trails. In addition to new parking, beach, and fishing facilities, remnant dune bluffs have been restored and revegetated.

Whihala Beach County Park, 1561 Park Road, Whiting. Travel Cline Avenue north to Riley Road, exit and follow park directional signs on Indianapolis Boulevard to 117th Street. Turn right on 117th to the park. A boat launch is open daily, from 4:30 a.m. to 7 p.m., from April through November. The Lake Michigan beach is open from 10 a.m. to 7 p.m. from Memorial Day through Labor Day.

Whihala Beach is easily accessible to a large resident population in Whiting/Robertsdale. It is also less than a half-hour from downtown Chicago.
Photo courtesy of the Lake County Parks Department.

Among the most frequent users of Whihala are boaters who work in nearby mills, many of whom are engineers or technically-trained people with limited time to play.
Photo courtesy of the Lake County Parks Department.

Gibson Woods Nature Preserve

The last sizable remnants of dune and swale topography in Lake County are contained in one hundred thirty acres known as Gibson Woods Nature Preserve. It is a unique spot for interpretive nature study that features self-guided trails, public programs, a learning center, and exhibits.

While all parks have nature at their cores, Gibson Woods focuses almost exclusively on nature, not only trees, woods, and animals of the wild, but historical artifacts of nature.

The Gibson Woods staff conducts a number of educational programs that are mini-adventures, programs that explore nature-related topics with hands-on activities. Emphasis is on recording experiences by keeping a journal of sketches and notes. Most of the time is spent outdoors, so participants must dress appropriately and bring insect repellent. Apart from a sketch pad or journal, all materials are provided by the staff. A certificate is awarded to anyone attending four or more sessions.

Gibson Woods Nature Preserve came into existence in 1981, with the dedication of one hundred twenty-nine acres of prime dune and swale prairie in Hessville (Hammond).

Gibson Woods consists of one hundred thirty acres of wild Lake County, the last big patch of dune and swale topography in Northwest Indiana. Photo by Joanna Shearer.

A bridge into adventure leads visitors into thick woods where nature without adornment can be studied, even on a wintery day. Photo by Jack Fusner.

Gibson Woods Nature Preserve,

6201 Parish Avenue, Hammond. Exit Cline Avenue in Hammond at 169th, travel west to Parish Avenue, turn north to Gibson Woods. Park is open from 9 a.m. to 5 p.m. daily. The Awareness Center is open from 11 a.m. to 5 p.m. daily.

Lake Etta County Park

With seventy acres of open space, Lake Etta County Park is a favorite fishing spot for anglers of all ages, and the lake is also popular with families for swimming and picnicking. The park features a stocked fishing lake, fish-cleaning station, fishing pier, bait sales and concessions, swimming

Lake Etta County Park, 4801 West 29th Avenue, Gary. Exit I-80/I-94 at Burr Street, travel south, then east on 29th Avenue to Lake Etta. Park is open from 7 a.m. until dusk the year round.

Lake Etta is a refreshing body of water that attracts families for a variety of recreations, including swimming, fishing, and boating.
Photo by Joanna Shearer.

beach with ramp, playground, picnic shelters, trails for walking, games, an exercise trail, and paddle boats.

Lake Etta is the site of the American Red Cross Basic Sailing course. Participants learn the skills necessary to take to the water with do-it-yourself experience taught by a certified instructor from the American Red Cross. Topics covered include all the working parts of a sailboat, different types of winds and how to use them, general safety, and much more. All participants who complete the course earn certification from the American Red Cross for Basic Sailing.

The program is open to people of all ages, however those under eighteen must have written consent from a parent or guardian. All participants are required to wear a life jacket that is provided during the program; each budding mariner sails for at least two hours each night. All participants must wear a swim suit and wear or bring a dry change of clothes and a towel, since they usually experience a couple of dunkings during the program. A waterslide complements the very popular swimming lake and beach.

Lake Etta came into being in 1977, when the Park Department assumed management of the lake under an inter-government agreement with the Indiana Department of Natural Resources. That agreement continued with the Little Calumet River Basin Development Commission, which, with the U.S. Army Corps of Engineers (Chicago District) and the Lake County Parks, broke ground for recreation opportunities at Lake Etta.

BAITING TAUGHT HERE

Many Lake County fisherpersons today dip their lines into inland lakes, including those in several Lake County Parks. The county even teaches effective fishing, especially at Oak Ridge Prairie, where the park provides poles and shows youngsters how to bait, cast, and reel in their lines. From April through October, Lake County parks provide put-and-take ponds stocked with catfish at Lemon Lake, Stoney Run, Oak Ridge Prairie, and Lake Etta.

One of the most popular fishing holes in Lake County, Lake Etta is so well stocked that lying has become a lost art in the lake's neighborhood. Photo by Joanna Shearer.

83

Oak Ridge Prairie County Park

Because of its natural diversity, Oak Ridge Prairie County Park serves up a rich variety of outdoor recreation activities. Among them are hikes on nature trails, cross-country skiing, sledding, and ice skating. Other park features include picnic shelters, hayrides, bonfires, and a fishing lake stocked with rainbow trout in spring and catfish throughout the summer. The person who can't refresh him/herself at Oak Ridge Prairie may be missing a pulse.

Oak Ridge Prairie is as popular in winter as at other times. One reason is the large sledding hill, complete with tube rentals. In addition, ice skating, cross-country ski trails, and ski rentals make Oak Ridge Prairie a great winter escape. If a visitor chooses a less strenuous mode, he or she may enjoy a winter stroll or peek at the varied wildlife making the park home. To wander about in Oak Ridge Prairie is to connect with the forces of life.

Located in Griffith near Hoosier Prairie, Oak Ridge Prairie's five hundred ninety-six acres are situated in the heart of Lake County. Preserved within the park's boundaries is a significant section of the mesic/wet prairie, one of several of the park's unique natural features.

The park is a favorite place for recreating throughout the year. While spending a quiet summer's morning fishing in the park's pond, visitors can hear the peaceful sounds of the grouses blowing in the wind. Well-stocked all year, the pond gives even the beginning fisherman a chance of catching the limit. There's plenty for the nature lover, too. Channelization of the marsh area has attracted a great number of wildlife and the miles of trails offer an ideal setting for serene beauty.

Oak Ridge Prairie County Park,

301 South Colfax Street, Griffith. The park is located southeast of Broad and Main Streets in Griffith. Travel Main Street to Colfax, turn south on Colfax for ½ mile to the park, which is open from 7 a.m. until dusk the year round.

Oak Ridge Prairie's proximity to trail corridors, existing and potential, lends itself to serving as a regional trail head. The Oak Savannah Trail, for example, starts at Oak Ridge Prairie and follows the abandoned E J & E right-of-way eleven miles to the Porter County Line. Other recent improvements include picnic and playground areas, hiking and equestrian trails, wetland restoration, and new interpretive facilities. Land acquisition has included 168.8 acres of valuable wetlands, uplands, and the Oak Savannah corridor.

Oak Ridge Prairie County Park opened in 1983.

Piscators start young at Oak Ridge Prairie Park, which contains one of the most fisher-friendly bodies of water in Lake County. Photo by Charles Temple.

The lake at Oak Ridge Prairie Park is so well stocked with trout and catfish that even a beginning fisherman can catch the limit allowed by law. Photo by Bob Bryerton.

Turkey Creek Golf Course

One of the most popular public golf courses in the Midwest, Turkey Creek has become even more attractive as a result of recent renovations of the clubhouse that increases banquet capacity. A new halfway house provides a restroom and concession facility conveniently located in the middle of the golf course. Other recent improvements include a well for irrigation and paving of the existing parking lot to accommodate increased golf course activities.

Turkey Creek Golf Course, 6400 Harrison Street, Merrillville. Exit I-65 and drive west on 61st Avenue to Harrison Street, then south for ¼ mile.

One reason for the popularity of Turkey Creek is that it not only tolerates but encourages small fry on the links. Throughout the summer, golf lessons for juniors are offered to youngsters from near and far. The resident golf pro instructs young golfers on the proper mechanics of the grip, swing, stance, putt, chip, and drive. Other matters addressed are club selection, rules of the game, and proper etiquette on the course.

An annual Junior Golf Tournament is held at Turkey Creek in late July. This competitive tournament is for golfers who are seventeen and eighteen years old; a novice division accommodates those sixteen and under.

Turkey Creek was dedicated as a county park in 1977.

The principal Potawatomi campsite in Lake County was just south of Turkey Creek, where the remains of a cemetery, workshop, and dancing grounds have been found. Today, the ground to the north is the Turkey Creek Golf Course, one of eleven county parks. Photo courtesy of Lake County Parks Department.

Deep River County Park

Comprising nine hundred sixty acres, Deep River County Park centers on Wood's Mill, built more than a century-and-a-half ago (about 1838) by John Wood of Massachusetts. Lake County's first industrialist, he established both the first gristmill and sawmill in the county. Beautifully restored today and open to the public, the

Deep River County Park, 9410 Old Lincoln Highway, Hobart. Travel U.S. 30 to Route 51, then north on Route 51 to the first stop sign, which is Old Lincoln Highway. Turn right (east) onto Old Lincoln Highway and drive 2½ miles to the park. It is located at the intersection of Old Lincoln Highway and County Line Road. The park is open from 7 a.m. until 10 p.m. from Memorial Day until Labor Day. The rest of the year, it is open from 7 a.m. until dusk.

building is connected to a water-powered wheel that harnesses the current of Deep River. Daily grain-grinding demonstrations in Wood's Mill are offered. Seasonal canoeing is available on Deep River. The park offers hiking trails, picnic shelters, hayrides, cross-country skiing, and an elaborate waterpark.

The old mill is also surrounded by a pond, a willow tree, several bridges, many beautiful flower beds, and a gazebo that has become the choicest place in the county to be married.

Wood's Mill provides visitors with a glimpse into the past, where corn is still ground between 4,000-pound stones to produce fresh, flavorful cornmeal, which can be bought, along with rag rugs and other mill souvenirs. Sifters and separators throughout the Mill demonstrate some of the many machines used in the gristmill. Other remnants of the past include an antique loom, a cider press, shoe repair machinery, quilts, and a replica photographer's studio.

On the third floor, Wood's Mill Gallery displays a variety of exhibits, including one in June that focuses on photographs of Lake County parks. Photographs entered in the contests are on exhibit seven days a week. July and August feature photographs taken by members of the Lake County Parks Photography Club.

John Wood's mill was the first mechanically driven mill in Lake County, and the only one for some three decades. Today, the mill and waterwheel are centerpieces of Deep River County Park and have been augmented by many other attractions. Photo by Joanna Shearer.

Special Deep River Attractions

Browsers have a field day at the Deep River County Park gift shop, where they find unique presents, foods, and historical merchandise. Contained in antique display cases and shelves that reach the ceiling, the items include miniatures, Hoosier and Wood's Mill souvenirs, toys, pottery, rugs, candies, jewelry, T-shirts, cassette tapes, CDs, collector tins, magnets, notecards, and postcards galore. The display appeals to several senses. Visitors can pick from large glass jars filled with colorful tasty rock candy sticks, while drinking a bottle of sasparilla. A hungry visitor can also buy jellies, honeys, teas, coffees, cocoas, fruit butters, pastas, sauces, mustards, and more. Large shelves hold cookbooks, history books, coloring books, paper doll books, nature guides, and children's story books. Even the camper can find what he or she is looking for, such as canteens, eating utensils, and cooking pots.

Among the special events at Deep River County Park, is Apple Day. It's a time in late September when apple cider, apple butter, taffy apples, and many other creations made with apples are available. Visitors can watch apple butter being made from different types of apples and spices in a big copper kettle over an open fire, stirred with a long-handled paddle. It takes many hours of cooking and stirring to boil the cider and cook the apples, adding just the right amount of spices for this very special treat: a thick, dark, sweet apple butter ladled into jars for storage.

Apple cider squeezed in an old cider

At the start of each spring, students flock to Deep River County Park for Maple Syrup Time. There they see a demonstration of the process of making maple syrup, from tapping the tree to boiling the sap at a perfect temperature. The finished maple syrup is bottled and sold in Deep River's Visitor Center.
Times *photo by Tracy Albano.*

press is also demonstrated, and in the Wood's Mill kitchen, volunteers prepare many delicious treats, such as apple jelly, applesauce, apple pies, Apple Brown Betty, and other desserts. Movies about apple cider-making and Johnny Appleseed are shown in the Visitor Center and the making of corn-husk and applehead dolls is demonstrated in the Mill. Meanwhile, children play old-fashioned games with old-fashioned toys, taking turns on old-fashioned stilts. Hayrides are also available, and several demonstrations take place, such as tomahawk throwing, quilting, and the use of the broad ax.

Another special event at Deep River County Park is maple syrup time. When the sap is running good during the first half of March, it is maple syrup time at Deep River. On weekends, staff and volunteers tap maple trees and collect the sap, which is then make into syrup in the evaporator of the Sugar House. Visitors can buy pure maple syrup at the Visitor Center, enjoy maple-iced doughnuts and other goodies, and watch the popular Maple Sugar Farmer.

Casey at the Bat

A time warp at Deep River County Park takes visitors back a century before multi-million-dollar baseball salaries, to watch the Deep River Grinders perform on weekends. A visitor can identify the Grinders because they wear black uniforms, shoes with no cleats, laced-up shirts, small-brimmed caps, and no gloves. Strikers (batters) use bats that look like axe handles and the umpire is dressed in a top hat and tails.

The catcher is called the "behind" and the pitcher is the hurler. There are no called balls or strikes, and a struck ball caught on one bounce, fair or foul, is an out. Because this is a gentleman's game, there is no argument from the players or the manager, should they disagree with the umpire's call. Nor is there swearing, spitting, or any other gauche behavior. Players address each other as Sir and a good play is greeted with a Huzzah or "Well done, Sir," by players and cranks (fans).

The Deep River Grinders play a full schedule of games both at home on Grinder Field, across Deep River from Wood's Gristmill, and away. They play teams with names like The Great Black Swamp Frogs, The Clodbusters, and The Rock Springs Ground Squirrels, as well as local teams made up of anyone willing to take a turn at the plate. Naturally, the Grinders play according to 1858 rules. Photo by Joanna Shearer.

Splashtastic

Although it is part of the Deep River County Park, the waterpark within it is popularly perceived as a separate county park. That's because the waterpark is the biggest attraction of all county parks in the summer.

Each year, the Lake County Parks and Recreation Department issues the public an invitation to enjoy what it calls a "splashtastic" good time at the waterpark. The facility simulates everything from crashing waves to the gentle current of a lazy stream and features, among other things, heated water, sand volley ball, waterslides, and picnic areas. For children, there's an interactive wet and dry play area where they can climb, slide, splash, and squirt to their heart's content. The staff assures that everyone has a good time, or at least a civil one.

Children can splash into a cool pool after a thrilling ride down a fast waterslide. Most recent of the Deep River

The Waterpark, which was added to Deep River County Park in the mid-1990s, has exceeded all expectations and is still growing, both in equipment and patronage. Photo by Joanna Shearer.

Waterpark additions is the "Dragon," a monstrous ride with two sixty-foot speed slides, the tallest, fastest, most thrilling ride at the park; the starting platform is higher than the canopy top of the Storm complex, another aquatic thrill. In an era that has given the world recreational parachuting and bunji jumping, those daring enough to try the Dragon can imagine they're free-falling to the ground, without the inconvenience of an unyielding stop. The sixty-foot fall takes just a few seconds and a lifetime of tingles.

Summertime's most popular attraction for children has become the waterpark at Deep River County Park. Photo by Joanna Shearer.

Lemon Lake County Park

Lemon Lake, with its two hundred ninety acres, is a popular place for family get-togethers and reunions, as well as ad hoc outings. Its features include lighted tennis courts, equipment rentals, basketball courts, hayrides, bonfires, softball diamonds and ball fields, a creative playground, cross-country skiing, and ice skating.

A pleasant piece of water that is as calm as an unfurrowed brow, Lemon Lake is suitable for paddle boating, row boating, and fishing, the lake being generously stocked. If one is up to a hike or wishes to take a turn around the lake on a bike, an asphalt trail is there for his or her use; the half-mile Touchstone Trail and the Vita Course are handicapped-accessible.

Lemon Lake County Park, 6322 W. 133rd Avenue, Crown Point. The park is located on 133rd Avenue, approximately ½ mile east of Cedar Lake. Travel Indiana 55 south to 133rd Avenue, then west for about three miles to the park entrance. The park is open from 7 a.m. until 10 p.m., from Memorial Day to Labor Day. It is open from 7 a.m. until dusk the rest of the year.

Lemon Lake is a lazy body of water, where people float in weightless leisure. Paddleboats and row boats are about as frenetic as it gets. Photo courtesy of the Lake County Parks Department.

Park users can take their pick of sports, including tennis under the lights, softball, soccer, basketball, and other exertions. In deference to contemporary lifestyles, a running track has been provided for those with a little 10-K in them. Photo courtesy of the Lake County Parks Department.

Buckley Homestead County Park

For those who wish to flash back to a time when farms in Lake County dominated life, there is no better site than the Buckley Homestead, which is an old-fashioned working farm kept alive in a world of cyberspace. Essentially, the restored 1900 farmhouse (and its outbuildings) is a museum, but it is much more. With its fifty acres of support and maintenance land, it is a working farm, but in the manner of many years ago. Thus, it is a history lesson.

The Buckley farm originated during the mid-1800s, when Dennis and Catherine Buckley immigrated to the United States from Ireland. They bought the original seventy-nine acre farm for fifty cents an acre from soldiers who had acquired the property as land grants. Alas, Dennis died only three years after coming to America, leaving his land and log house to his children. Son John bought his brother's share of the property and built the present house in the late 1800s. John's son, Charles, farmed some of the land, but concentrated on raising Holstein cows, milking them by hand and selling the milk in Chicago. In 1977, the Homestead that had supported three generations of Buckleys was donated to the Lake County Parks and Recreation Department by Rose Buckley Pearce, great-granddaughter of Dennis and Catherine Buckley.

Today, visitors find a combination of traditional farm activities and animals, as well as historical background of early farming life. They also find an abundance of special activities and festivals. The best-known of these is Buckley Homestead Days in the fall, which provides visitors with an educational look at the way it was. Traditional crafts, such as weaving, tatting, spinning, quilting, basket making, corn husk dolls, bobbin lace, and more are demonstrated with several items offered for sale. Skills such as whittling, woodworking, cabinet making, and blacksmithing are also demonstrated. Early steam and gas engine farm equipment are on hand with proud owners of the rare pieces ready to share their knowledge. And there's plenty to entertain the kids, especially farm animals. The one-room schoolhouse is also an attraction, although less entertaining to kids than the animals.

In the days before radio, television, and talkies, audiences listened to high-profile figures live and in person. The vehicle that made this possible was the Chautauqua, which went on the road from its home base in western New York. Such a traveling Chautauqua, shown here, is recreated at Buckley Homestead, where the themes seem unchanged by the passage of time and fads. Photo by Joanna Shearer.

Buckley Homestead County Park,

3606 Belshaw Road, Lowell, Exit I-65 at Route 2 and drive east through Lowell about four miles to Hendricks Road, then south for ¼ mile. The park is open from 7 a.m. until dusk the year round. Buildings open weekends from 10 a.m. until 5 p.m.

Buckley is a living history farm depicting life as it was in the past. Photo by Leo Ranachowski.

One of the popular features of the Buckley Homestead County Park is the hayride, shown here, which is somewhat smoother than in days of yore because of tires on the wheels. Photo by Joanna Shearer.

Grand Kankakee Marsh County Park

The nine hundred thirty acre Grand Kankakee Marsh County Park offers a variety of activities for the outdoor sportsperson. Seasonal waterfowl, dove and deer hunting, fishing, hiking, and picnicking serve the public, and there's more to come.

Grand Kankakee Marsh County Park, 21690 Range Line Road, Hebron. Exit I-65 at Route 2 and drive east to Range Line Road (Clay Street); turn south for five miles. The park is open from 7 a.m. until dusk, from January to September.

Located on an erstwhile hunters' and fishers' paradise that once was the largest marsh in the nation, the Grand Kankakee Marsh County Park continues to be a wonderful place for outdoors people, horse people, and those who would generally soak in nature.

In the early nineteenth century, few settlers ever saw the Kankakee River, shown here, because it was subsumed by the Great Kankakee Marsh, which was about five miles wide with water several feet deep much of the year. The Marsh country was a paradise for hunters, who not infrequently showed up from Europe. Photo by Joanna Shearer.

To help people enjoy the park to its maximum, the park department conducts a series of workshops. In mid-September, it sponsors the Indiana Department of Natural Resources' Hunter Education Class, which consists of a minimum of ten hours of classroom instruction. Subjects covered include: firearms and ammunition, proper handling of firearms and bows, wildlife conservation, hunter responsibilities, and wildlife management principles.

Another teaching mechanism that fits the locale is an introductory canoe clinic. It is designed to teach the beginning canoeist how to use the seven basic paddle strokes, explain and demon-

strate the basic equipment used in canoeing, provide on-the-water practice in the canoes, provide information on where to canoe in Indiana, and present a segment on wilderness canoeing and how to outfit one's self for such an experience. Participants see a slide presentation and receive printed material to take home with them.

Instruction in the use of canoes ties in nicely to the park's emphasis on voyageurs who once plied the Kankakee. Each spring, the park sponsors a Voyageurs' Rendezvous, co-sponsored by the Kankakee Alliance, Moses Hazens Company of Major Scott's Provisional Battalion, and Lake County Parks. The rendezvous is a reenactment of a long lost romantic era on the Kankakee. Reenactors fall out in the dressiest of costumes and visitors to the park are invited to join in the reenactment.

Voyageurs plied the Kankakee country to trade dry goods and trinkets to Native Americans for fur pelts. Occasionally they stopped for a rendezvous, at which time they would engage in contests of skill and strength. Such gatherings, shown here, are reenacted each spring at the Grand Kankakee Marsh County Park, complete with authentic canoes, tents, games, songs, and the like. Photo by Jack J. Fusner.

Three Rivers County Park

In August of 1999, the Lake County Parks Department broke ground for an eleventh park designed to be the eastern recreation anchor to the Little Calumet Flood Control and Recreation Project. Eventually, this park will preserve a corridor along the Little Calumet River, Burns Waterway, and Deep River.

Three Rivers County Park is located on the Gary/Lake Station border. It abuts the Deep River Outdoor Education Center, a Gary School City property where outdoor education classes are taught. The new park, located south of I-80/94 just east of I-65, has easy access from the major highways.

The new construction includes a one hundred seventy car parking lot and a paved hiking/biking trail around a thirty-eight-acre lake. Future amenities will include a visitors' center, picnic shelters, wet and dry playground facilities, a gatehouse, and a boat dock. Programs at the park will include fishing, sailboating, and kayaking.

Beginners in sailing can gain instruction at Three Rivers County Park, where they can learn the basics of pushing and pulling combined with balance. Safety, rigging, launching, and tactics are taught in instructional classes for students as young as two years old. All participants must be able to swim a short distance while wearing a life preserver.

While still in a state of incompletion, the new Three Rivers County Park was already attracting fishers and sailboaters, shown here. Photo by Joanna Shearer.

Stoney Run County Park

In addition to being a most agreeable site for fishing, cross-country skiing, hiking, and other outdoor activities, Stoney Run County Park is the site of the county's Vietnam Memorial. It also holds a number of special events, including, for a number of years, an annual Bluegrass Festival, which was appropriate since Bill Monroe, inventor of bluegrass, once worked in the barrelhouse of the Sinclair Refinery in East Chicago.

Stoney Run County Park, 142nd and Union Street, Leroy. Exit I-65 at Route 231 and travel east about seven miles to Hebron and follow the signs to the park. The park is open from 7 a.m. until dusk the year round.

Just for the kids (regardless of age), Stoney Run County Park features clowns to enhance the fun. The clowns hold forth on the relatively new playground at the park, which also features a "Flush 'ern," a new style of dunk tank, as well as games, prizes, face painting, and many other surprises.

Stoney Run is also the starting and ending point for a "Pedal the Parks" program. The rally begins and ends at Stoney Run in late August and consists of rides of 25, 15, and 10 miles. Everyone follows the same course, although the 25-mile route is from Stoney Run to the Grand Kankakee Marsh and back. Water stations exist throughout and a snack stop halfway into the 25-mile ride. Special arrangements are made for those interested in a 50-mile ride.

Stoney Run County Park came into existence when, in 1972, the park board bought four hundred acres near Leroy. In 1973, Stoney Run County Park became the second park in the Lake County system.

Stoney Run County Park is home to the Vietnam Veteran's Memorial. Photo by Charles Temple.

BIKING

Pedal the (Lake County) Parks includes a Trail Blaze bike race of approximately five miles around the perimeter trail of Stoney Run, in addition to a ten-, twenty-five-, and fifty-mile Bike Rally. These events usually involve all-terrain bicycles and require helmets. The rally begins and ends at Stoney Run County Park. The Trail Blaze is one race in a four-race series co-sponsored with the Munster Park Department.

While the series is competitive, it doesn't preclude beginning riders, since the scoring system is set up to accommodate all ages and abilities. Participants may ride in each individual race or join the series competition. Series awards are based on a low point system that emphasizes consistency, therefore riders don't even have to win an individual race to win the series.

The last race in the series is Mount Trashmore at Lakewood Park in Munster. Corporate sponsors include Schwinn Cycling and Fitness, Pepsi, and Family Mobile Medical Services, Inc. Also on hand to provide expert guidance about cycling is Team Ameritech's Midwest Regional Woman's Elite Team.

chapter 6

The Complex

The epicenter of entertainment in today's Lake County is the Merrillville complex that includes the Radisson Hotel at Star Plaza. The hotel contains three hundred forty-seven guest rooms and suites; six restaurants and lounges; a tropical atrium with a pool, whirlpool, and sauna; an exercise room; outdoor pools; and a convention center with thirty thousand feet of flexible meeting space. The Star Plaza Theatre has three thousand four hundred cushioned seats, perfect acoustics, and no location farther from the stage than one hundred ten feet.

By way of satisfying many appetites, the hotel provides luxury accommodations, plus a lobby and atrium with a tropical island theme. It is a Northern Indiana marvel known for its Southern hospitality. Beautiful and romantic, the hotel offers patrons fine dining; in less formal moments, they also can have a pre-concert cocktail right in the lobby, at the Khaki Club, an attractive open lounge.

The lobby/atrium contains hot tubs, waterfalls, and macaw birds, which makes visiting it seem like going to the South Seas. And just a few steps away is the Star Plaza Theatre, packed with people watching a top-rated show. All-in-all, the complex is a refreshing change-of-pace, a getaway where a person can escape and refuel, a rare place, unrivaled in the nation. Out-of-town theatrical producers who know a thing or two about the lapidary art have referred to the Radisson Hotel at Star Plaza complex as a gem, while awed observers of a younger generation have sometimes called it an entertainment planet.

One of the top twenty-five concert venues in the world, the Star Plaza welcomes to its stage the most renowned entertainers of the day, some of whom make regular stops at the facility. Entertainers range from such classic comedians as Bob Hope and Phyllis Diller to sumptuous opera companies, from Bob Fosse's Broadway

amusements

One of the best twenty-five pop concert venues in the world, the Star Plaza features top-name performers and shows throughout the year. Photo courtesy of the Lake County Convention and Visitors Bureau.

dancers and Tom Jones' seductive gyrations to the eternal doo-opping of Stormy Weather. Other entertainers among thousands have included the Moody Blues, Pam LaBelle, Wynonna, Bobby Dylan, and B. B. King, collectively representing every type of talent extant. The theatre has even staged an ice show. In all, the Star Plaza presents at least one hundred thirty performances each year, attracting a combined audience of more than a half million.

The Radisson Hotel at Star Plaza has been honored in a variety of ways. For example, virtually every year the Star Plaza is nominated for theater-of-the-year award by *Performance* magazine. The hotel-auditorium complex has also won VISTA awards for achievement and tourism promotion; such awards are given to organizations and individuals that best promote Indiana as a travel destination. The Radisson won in the category of "Advertising and Promotional Materials for a Restaurant or Lodging Establishment." Significantly, it has won the Radisson Hotels International President's Award.

With three hundred forty-seven rooms and its own in-house convention center, the hotel offers packages to suit almost any taste or budget. Its operators have been able to neatly combine the hotel with food and beverage for any and all occasions, not only in conjunction with the theater, but separately, many people booking rooms for weekend respites.

Lodging

More than three thousand first-rate hotel and motel rooms exist in Lake County and the number grows every year. Since competing innkeepers have discovered that success is spelled c-o-o-p-e-r-a-t-i-o-n, there has been a trend in recent years to provide a county-wide standard of extra comfort and services so as to make a visitor's stay a pleasant, even memorable one.

Most of the hotels and motels are members of national or regional chains, but the ownership is local. Most cluster near expressways, convenient to entertainment, industry, and airports. Large hotel complexes house conventions in meeting space comparable to the most modern anywhere. Some hotels offer luxury appointments. All are suitable for family holidays, weekend visits, or overnight stays. As a general rule, prices paid for lodging in Lake County are much lower than those paid in Chicago and its Illinois suburbs.

The Radisson represents a total escape for guests, who might think they are on a tropical island, instead of Merrillville. Here, two guests splash around in a pool beneath a waterfall in the atrium of the hotel. Photo by Patricia Young McKinlay.

Above: The Radisson Hotel brings the outdoors indoors with a lobby and atrium that features good food and drink in a setting that includes a pool fed by a babbling waterfall, augmented by sounds of the wilds, including real birds. Photo courtesy of the Lake County Convention and Visitors Bureau.

Typical of the many fine hotels and motels in Lake County, La Quinta Inn features a heated pool and rooms with rich decor, bright bathrooms, plush carpeting, built-in closets, and 25-inch television sets with first-run movies on demand, as well as the latest video game. Photo courtesy of the Lake County Convention and Visitors Bureau.

Dining

Driven by a large population of early retirees, Lake County is an eating-out sort of place, which has generated many restaurants catering to the desires of this expanding market. As a result, a person can find any kind of restaurant to suit his tastes, needs, and budget, from fast food to ethnic repasts to fine dining.

One of the largest and most modern restaurants in Lake County today, Teibel's began in 1929 as essentially a place in the country to get good chicken dinners. And how could anyone beat the price? Photo courtesy of Art Schweitzer.

Nationally-known Phil Smidt's in Whiting/Robertsdale is famous for its frog legs and its boned-and-buttered perch, which are served on heroic, all-you-can-eat platters, unless the patron specifies a smaller portion. Photo by Richard D. Rudzinski.

Above: No shortage of elegant restaurants exists in Lake County, where visitors can be pampered to the limits of their credit cards. Photo courtesy of the Lake County Convention and Visitors Bureau.

Left: The elegant Ramada Inn and Dynasty Conference Center in North Hammond runs the gamut of eating out. The banquet and meeting rooms accommodate up to six hundred people, while Johnel's Restaurant, a family eatery, offers an extensive menu of superb food at modest prices. Photo courtesy of the Lake County Convention and Visitors Bureau.

Movies

Most of the magnificent movie palaces of the 1920s are long gone, but one of that ilk in Whiting has not only survived but been resurrected. Hailed in 1924 when it opened as the most beautiful

and comfortable theater in Northwest Indiana, the Hoosier featured an exquisite exterior of terra-cotta relief work that echoed the classic detailed interior. Its rich furnishings, detailed plaster work, and tasteful color scheme inspired the appellation "House Beautiful." And its innovative refrigeration system (air conditioning) was matched by only a few other theaters in the Midwest.

In addition to silent movies, the Hoosier

Theaters in Whiting have a long history, and all resided on 119th Street. First there was the Star Theater, then a more elaborate one called the Princess, and then a fancier one yet called the Capitol. Finally, during the flush days of the twenties, the most baroque of them all debuted in 1924: the Hoosier, with trolley service right to the door. Painting by Al Odlivak.

became an important venue for national vaudeville and stage circuits. It therefore presented such acts as Sam and Henry (Amos and Andy), played by Freeman Gosten and Charles Correll. When young Charles Laughton arrived in America from England, he played the Hoosier. So did W. C. Fields, the Three Stooges, and other still-recognizable names.

The Hoosier was brought back to life in most of its original glory by John Katris and his family, who spent two years restoring the theater. The family did so in such particular detail that John, because he had been painting gilt on the ceiling while lying on his back, became known as the Michaelangelo of Lake County.

Among other smaller theaters that have weathered the storm of television and multiplexes are the Town in Highland, which serves pastries between features, and the Art in Hobart.

The Art Theater in Hobart attracts a steady clientele of people who want to get out of the house to see a good film in a real theater, but do so at an affordable price. Ed Prusiecki, shown here, is the very active senior citizen who owns the Art and makes good, inexpensive entertainment possible in Hobart and vicinity. Times *photo by Aldino Gallo.*

Casinos

Lake County has become Greater Chicago's most popular location for special amusements and entertainment, mainly because of four floating casinos moored close to each other along the Lake Michigan shoreline. Millions of visitors each year cruise The Big Lake on these opulent palaces, which also feature fine dining and lively entertainment. Patrons can engage in games that range from baccarat to blackjack and just about everything in between. Many who crowd the tables package their gaming with an overnight stay at a Lake County Hotel.

Together, the four boats feature more than one hundred forty thousand square feet of Las Vegas excitement. Some five thousand four hundred slot machines and two hundred sixty-eight table games are available to patrons. Afterwards, players may partake of a four-star dinner at any of the gaming pavilions. Each features a fine dining restaurant as well as magnificent buffet-style dining. Boarding times for each vessel vary and reservations are prudent during peak hours.

Harrah's Casino East Chicago has perhaps the most colorful stage of the four casinos, and the one that requires the attention of more experts. Shown here working on the hydraulic lift are George Doppier of Hyre Electric in Highland, Turan Tekin, of Kern Sculpture in New Orleans, and David Fry of ABC Construction in Memphis. Times photo by Tracy Albano.

Sailing out of Gary's Buffington Harbor are the Trump Casino and the Majestic Star Casino, which began to operate in 1996. The two hundred eighty-eight-foot Trump Casino, named for New York financier and gaming mogul Donald Trump, is a luxurious vessel with room for twenty-five hundred passengers. The Majestic Star Casino, a three hundred eight-foot converted dinner-cruise ship, can accommodate as many as fifteen hundred passengers. The two hundred eighty-eight-foot Empress Casino sails from the Hammond Marina, and Harrah's Casino East Chicago, a three hundred eighty-eight-foot, three thousand seven hundred fifty passenger boat, the largest of the four, sails out of Indiana Harbor, near Pastrick Marina.

In addition to providing an amusement resource, the boats have also generated by-products that directly and indirectly raise the level of leisure fare in Lake County. Tourist dollars attracted into Lake County, along with tax revenues, have encouraged a great deal of construction and real estate development, which, in turn, has generated many jobs, increased the tax base, and generally encouraged ever more and better amusements throughout the county.

Below: Donald Trump's two hundred eighty-eight-foot Trump Casino is a truly lavish vessel with room for twenty-five hundred passengers. Visitors may stay at a luxurious new hotel overlooking Lake Michigan. The hotel is just steps from Trump Casino and minutes from Downtown Chicago. Image courtesy of Shelton Fritsch DDM.

Above: One-armed bandits galore provide patrons with a bit of diversion on the four casino boats. Here a woman on the Empress Casino has apparently hit a jackpot on a 25 cent machine. Photo courtesy of the Empress Casino Hammond.

A three hundred and eight-foot converted dinner-cruise ship, the Majestic Star Casino can accommodate as many as fifteen hundred passengers. It sails out of Buffington Harbor (Gary), and provides free shuttle service from most Lake County hotels. Photo courtesy of the Lake County Convention and Visitors Bureau.

The two hundred eighty-eight-foot Empress is shown nestling up to its pavilion just south of the Hammond Marina, and just a mile from the Chicago city line. A special ramp leads to and from the boat to accommodate cars that exit the Chicago Skyway/Indiana Toll Road. Photo courtesy of Carle Communications.

Built in 1940 by Inland Steel and turned over to East Chicago as a gift, Block Stadium has hosted the best in baseball that has been offered locally. Prior to African-Americans breaking the color line of major league baseball, all the stars of the Negro League played at Block Stadium. Photo by Patricia Young McKinlay.

Spectator Sports

More than one observer has said that the two main preoccupations of Lake County are politics and sports. While a lot of questions could be raised about the former, there's no argument about the latter. Lake County is a hotbed of all sports: football, basketball, baseball, and others. People flock to see teams—most of them high school—as if they were champions of the world, and sometimes they almost are.

Below: Ray P. Gallivan Field, seen here in the distance, is a relatively new football facility where Whiting High plays its games. It is one of a number of similar facilities in Lake County, the largest being Merrillville High's stadium. Photo by Richard D. Rudzinski.

In the late-nineteenth century and throughout the twentieth century, amateur baseball was Lake County's chief adult spectator sport. Each town had a favorite team. When the sport was interrupted by World War II and almost expired, the person responsible for reviving it after the war was Chris Platis, shown here. Photo courtesy of the East Chicago Hall of Fame.

When unsung Hammond Tech emerged from their makeshift, boiler room gym to win the Indiana basketball championship in 1940, fifty thousand people showed up the next day in downtown Hammond to welcome the heroes back from Indianapolis. Photo courtesy of Art Schweitzer.

The Genesis Convention Center in Gary is so versatile it can accommodate a rodeo, shown here, or a major banquet. For dinner, the facility can serve up to twenty-five hundred guests. *Times* photo by Wes Pope.

Built in the mid–1930s, Hammond's Civic Center has hosted high school basketball tournaments, home games of a professional basketball team, boxing matches, professional wrestling matches, banquets, choral groups, country dancing, and just about every other popular amusement the mind can conjure up. Shown here is an elephant being led out of the Civic Center during a circus. *Times* photo by Zbigniew Bzdak.

Popular Amusements

Facing page, top: The number one spectator sport in America is said to be motor car racing, a version of which is found at the Illiana Motor Speedway in Schererville. The track opened as a half-mile oval in 1948 in an erstwhile cornfield that included part of a World War II airstrip. Although it began as a motorcycle track, it soon accommodated Indy race car drivers with names like Foyt, Parson, Rutman, Rutherford, Bentenhauser, and others. Times photo by Wes Pope.

Celebration Station, the only one of its kind in North America, caters to small fry, who practically exhaust the place. The twelve-acre facility comprises eighty carts, miniature golf, batting cages, a kids' roller coaster, an arcade, large restaurants and much more. It is located in Merrillville near Century Mall. Photo courtesy of the Lake County Convention and Visitors Bureau.

A Hammond High graduate of 1928, Edwin "Eddie" Nelson returned to his city as a coach and school administrator. He is shown here with two important spectator venues, the Hammond High football field in the foreground and the Civic Center in the background. PhotoCalumet image by Linda Dorman-Gainer.

Fests, Events, and Celebrations

Lake County is a non-stop fest. Every change of season brings a bounty of festivals, ethnic and otherwise, which provide a diversity of experiences the year round. The range is remarkable: a reenactment of a Civil War battle, a concert by a German marching band, a rich-smelling Greek festival, a traditional African dance, and more—all help extract what little boredom there is from the year.

Fall means the Harvest Moon Festival and Buckley Homestead Days, which recovers the excitement and tradition of the yearly harvest. Cold weather brings the wonder of "Winter Magic," which features an ice carving competition in Munster and several winter activities for the whole family. And summer means, among many others, Fourth of July celebrations, some lasting several days.

Since fest is another way of saying feast, each event offers more food than anyone should eat, including traditional Old Country peasant cuisine that has changed hardly at all in more than a century. The taste and smell of roast lamb, burritos, pierogi, frankfurters, prase, janjetlina, sarmale, kielbasa and kiska, dulma, blodpoise, egg rolls, shish ke bob, and many more savories blend uniquely with fest sights and sounds that almost overload a person's senses. Some fests or events have an athletic basis, as in the annual Gus Macker 3-on-3 Charity Basketball Tournament, which is but one of a number of amateur events held year round, both outside and inside. Whether it's bowling, track and field, or a triathlon, though, the feat and the feast can be found in Lake County in abundance.

Hardly any special event in Lake County is without a clown to help kids look like someone else, as is the case here. Success is measured very simply. If a boy can recognize himself in a mirror, the clown has failed. Photo courtesy of the Lake County Convention and Visitors Bureau.

Below: Pumpkin festivals are as indigenous to Lake County in the fall as wine fests are to France. Here a girl joins the fun at the County Line Orchard's annual Pumpkin Festival. Photo courtesy of the Lake County Convention and Visitors Bureau.

The biggest event of the year is the Lake County Fair, where farmers and 4-Hers vie for blue in husbandry, preserves, sunflowers, and everything else associated with farm life. And then there's time to party, as a midway pops up full of games and rides, shown here. Photo courtesy of Edda Taylor Photographic.

Civil War reenactments have become a traditional feature of Buckley Homestead Days, in Lowell. Here a sergeant urges a group of recruits to form a straight line. Significantly, Lake County sent many of its finest young men right off the farm to that most slaughterous of wars. Times *photo by John J. Watkins.*

The Medicine Show that was so much a part of traveling entertainments is one of several reenactments of the past that are features of Buckley Homestead Days. Photo by Larry A. Brechner.

Arguably the most popular fest of the year in Lake County, the Pierogi Fest in Whiting crowns a Mr. Pierogi, whose title carries more prestige than a homecoming queen's. Joe Kus held the honor in the Pierogi parade shown here. Photo courtesy of the Whiting Chamber of Commerce.

The biggest parade and the most spectacular fireworks occur in Whiting on the Fourth of July, where the floats sometimes resemble landmarks. Times photo by Zbigniew Bzdak.

According to a newspaper poll, D. C. Country Junction and Zoo in Lowell is Lake County's best "Western Bar and Live Entertainment." Dancers of country and western music do their thing on a floor that is the largest of its kind in the United States. Everything is live. The Junction features two bands, dancing, dance lessons, two giant cook-your-own grills, bingo, and a zoo that houses exotic and endangered animals. There's also an arcade area, ice cream shop, and gift shop.

Among special events at the Junction have been the world championship Great Midwest Rodeo Tour.

The overall facility is available for corporate barbecues, children's birthday parties, barn weddings, fund-raisers, school events, and country and western fashion shows, to name a few. *Times* photo by Wes Pope.

119

chapter 7

The Center

What was once considered elitist in Lake County is now enjoyed and appreciated by the general public through the Center for the Visual and Performing Arts in Munster. Set in a luxuriant formal garden, the Center houses the Indiana Symphony Orchestra headquarters, art and photo galleries, dining rooms for four hundred fifty people, a gift shop, and the Northern Indiana Arts Association.

The Northern Indiana Arts Association (NIAA) has branches in other Lake County communities. The first of these satellites was the Hammond Branch, which occupies the former Northern Indiana Public Service Co. building. This branch offers educational programs, job training for young artists, conventions focusing on comic art as an occupation, and graffiti gatherings designed to draw youths off the street and channel their creativity toward positive ends. Even the exterior of the Hammond center features graffiti murals.

Murals in Lake County have a long history, peaking in the 1930s when the federal government paid artists to paint onto public buildings. Depression art adorns several buildings in Lake County, the most accessible being murals in the Crown Point and Hobart post offices, which were paid for by the Treasury Department.

The Crown Point mural illustrates Solon Robinson, the putative founder of Crown Point, interacting with the Indians as settlers come streaming into Lake County with the tacit approval of the aborigines. A similar, though later, scene adorns the Hobart post office. It is supposed to represent how Hobart looked in 1870. So viewers see an early trading post and post office combination, a blacksmith shop, a gristmill, a sawmill, and an Indian squaw sitting on the trading post steps, while her husband bargains with the storekeeper.

The mural in the East Chicago Pastrick Branch library is less literal, having enough symbolism in it for several buildings. It's a WPA painting (not Treasury) and is replete with Grecian costumes, pillars, radios, newspapers, a picture of President Franklin Delano Roosevelt, and a palm branch. The artist used local models and even local garb,

arts

Morrie Johnson of Merrillville and Beverly Hills, California, displays a bronze head of his sailing partner, Marv Gordon of Chicago. Photo by Richard D. Rudzinski.

Most cities of Lake County conduct annual art fairs at which local artists can display and sell their wares and compete for prizes. Shown here is Lee Senovic, who won a blue ribbon at the Hobart Art Fair. Photo by Patricia Young McKinlay.

like the band uniforms of E. C. Washington High School. The most transfixing elements in the mural, however, are pretty girls wearing classical Grecian gowns topped with 1935 hairdos.

A more recent example of art in public places is the "Man of Steel," created in 1976 by Hermann Gurfinkel and located in Hammond's Harrison Park. Inland Steel (now Ispat Inland) donated 16,019 pounds of sheet plate, I-beams, and angles for the massive sculpture. The abstraction of a human head weighs ten tons and looms twenty-two feet above a three-foot-high concrete plinth. Gurfinkel also sculpted the "Reader" at the Lake County Library in Merrillville, a seven-foot piece that would be ten feet tall if standing.

The importance of art in Lake County can also be found in the conversion of Gary Emerson High School into a fine arts high school. The only one of its kind in Indiana, Emerson is a public school where students can be thoroughly immersed in the arts while completing a high school degree. All other schools in Lake County offer art, too, usually as an elective.

In some cases, art links a community institution with the overall community. For example, the Gallery Northwest, located in Gary, provides arts programs and exhibitions as a link between Indiana University Northwest and the community.

Facing Page: The massive "Man of Steel" in Hammond's Harrison Park is Lake County's most notable contribution to public art. Sculpted by Hermann Gurfinkle, the abstracted human head is twenty-two feet high and weighs ten tons. Photo courtesy of Carle Communications.

One of the great successes in changing behavior from destructive to constructive has been the painting of murals by young people. A few years ago, such murals were considered graffiti and scorned; today, the urge to paint walls is channeled with beautiful results, both as art and as social behavior. Photo courtesy of Tom Hocker.

Marion J. "Pablo" Culp, shown here on one of his sailboats, epitomizes the uninhibited eclecticism of Lake County artists. So accomplished at daubing oil on canvas that he once was named best-in-class artist in the Midwest, he also paints billboards and murals of heroic scale. Mostly, though, he skims across Lake Michigan and the Gulf of Mexico, once sailing all the way to Cuba to buy a decent cigar. Photo by Patricia Young McKinlay.

Zivko Zic, an artist who paints with wet, thick oil paint, elevates the commonplace to an aesthetic level. Shown here is a piece from his one-man show at the Art Gallery of Gary's main library, entitled "Steel, Light and Form: Industrialscapes of the American Rust Belt." Zic's work has been likened to plein air (French impressionalist) painting of the late–nineteenth century. Photo courtesy of Claude Zic.

The Northern Indiana Arts Association headquarters at the Center, its activities including exhibits, classes, lectures, readings, and bus tours. Each June it also presents a Festival of Arts that is free to the public. Photo courtesy of the Center for the Visual and Performing Arts.

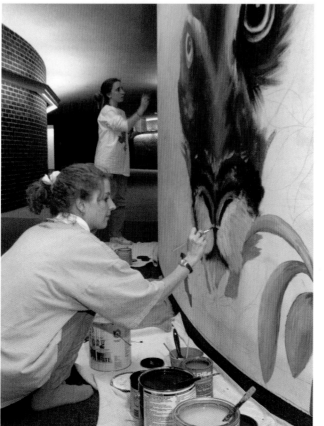

Susan Hults, front, one of Lowell High School's art teachers, and senior Sarah Hoshaw work on a new mural for one of the circular walls at the high school. The mural features wild animals from around the world and complements an existing mural featuring aquatic animals. Times photo by John J. Watkins.

125

Theater

The Center for Visual and Performing Arts is, essentially, the professional playhouse of Lake County, where seasoned actors appear regularly in "Theater At The Center." In addition to plays, the Center is taken over by Indiana Symphony Orchestra for several performances, highlighted by seasonal concerts.

A number of highly-talented community groups also perform throughout the county, which inspired the appellation "As Far As It Gets Off Broadway." One of the oldest continuous community groups is the Marian Theatre Guild of Whiting/Robertsdale. Founded in 1928, the Guild began as the St. John Drama Group, an ensemble that performed in Slovak for immigrants in the neighborhood, where there were more Slovaks than in most foothill towns of the White Carpathians. Although religious motifs dominated early dramas, the company gradually became so thoroughly Americanized that today it presents the best of Broadway, sometimes better than Broadway presents it.

The Genesius Guild, named for Saint Genesius, patron of actors, was founded in 1984 by members of Hammond's First United Methodist Church. As it grew into a community theater group, it added non-church members to its company. At first the Genesius Guild presented familiar musicals. Gradually, though, the

Community Theater groups in Lake County tend to favor show business standards. Shown here is a production of "Hello Dolly," which more than one community group has staged.
Photo by Larry A. Brechner.

The Northwest Indiana Opera Theater group surfaces from time to time to stage musicals and light opera. Here is a scene from its version of "Brigadoon." Photo by Larry A. Brechner.

Guild expanded to include non-musical plays, Children's Theater, Youth Theater, pantomime, interactive murder mysteries, musical reviews, and original works.

Prior to 1961, Indiana University Northwest imported a few plays from the IU drama department in Bloomington. However, when an ensemble of five local actors appeared in a production of "Bell, Book and Candle," the "Theatre At Indiana University Northwest" was born. That ad hoc start inspired a Bachelor of Arts degree program at IUN, which began in 1974. Today, the theater operates with an entirely IUN cast and offers professionally-mounted productions worthy of the largest university. Plays are chosen to give both theater majors and patrons a season of representative plays from various periods and styles of theater. A favorite is the annual Children's Theater production that has exposed more than three hundred thousand children to live theater experiences.

The Marian Theatre Guild usually presents two shows a year at the St. John complex in Whiting/Robertsdale. A comedy, uncomplicated drama, or modest musical is presented in the spring, while a full-scale musical takes over the stage in the fall. Photo courtesy of the Whiting Chamber of Commerce.

Music

Perhaps the art with the deepest roots in Lake County is music, which has also been diverse. At its most basic, music tradition in Lake County draws on such ethnic groups as the Croatian Peradovic Choir; Karageorge Serbian Singing Society; Chopin Chorus of the Polish Singers Alliance; Welsh Cambrian Society; and others. Churches, which are many and diverse, present outstanding choirs of their own, some of which still sing in the vernacular.

At various times, special groups emerge to perform more normative fare. U.S. Steel once had a famous men's chorus that performed at venues far beyond the bounds of Lake County. The East Chicago Male Chorus and the East Chicago Farrar (female) Chorus, each with fifty members, also sang far and wide. And presently, Chorus Angelorum in Whiting/Robertsdale presents an annual fall concert that features soloists from Chicago's Lyric Opera.

Everyone in the intimate auditorium of the Center for the Visual and Performing Arts is just a few feet away from the performance or the performer. The circular stage and seating arrangement is especially suited for concerts by individuals. Photo courtesy of the Center for the Visual and Performing Arts.

The champion Orak Pipe and Drums began in Hammond and now is headquartered in Michigan City. Photo by Patricia Young McKinlay.

Instrumental music was built on a foundation of German bands, which catered to the tastes of the people who early-on dominated Lake County. Until World War I, a number of towns in Lake County had town bands, some had lodge bands, and the affection for instrumental music carried into the school system. Whiting once had a boys' group known as Father Lach's Band that, on the eve of World War II, toured Europe. At least three Lake County High Schools—Hammond, Whiting, and Hobart—have won contests that crowned them the best band in the United States.

This interest in instrumental music spilled over into orchestras, resulting in several of them winning high laurals. The Calumet Symphony Orchestra, which was affiliated with the Calumet Center of Indiana University, was an extension of various musical groups in East Chicago and Indiana Harbor. Likewise, the Gary Symphony Orchestra coalesced various musical groups. Both the Calumet and Gary organizations and others have now blended into The Indiana Symphony Orchestra and Chorus, a professional group that is perhaps the finest of its type outside a major city.

Beyond the purely ethnic and classical, Lake County's passion for music has produced a number of jazz and pop artists. One need only note Michael Jackson of Gary, who is more decorated than a Christmas tree.

Another all-purpose venue that holds musical programs is Gary's stunning looking Genesis Center, designed by architect Wendell Campbell. Photo by Richard D. Rudzinski.

Possibly the finest regional orchestra and chorus in America, the Indiana Symphony Orchestra presents both a classical series and a pops series at the Star Plaza Theater, and a chamber series at the Center for Visual and Performing Arts. Photo courtesy of the Indiana Symphony Orchestra.

The Indiana Symphony Orchestra plays most of its full-orchestra concerts at the Star Plaza in Merrillville, and most of its chamber music concerts at the Center for the Visual and Performing Arts in Munster. It also performs situational concerts throughout Lake County, such as an annual summer series in Whiting Park. Photo courtesy of the Whiting Chamber of Commerce.

Above: Although it is used for every type of entertainment imaginable, Hammond's Civic Center also holds popular concerts of the day. Photo by Richard D. Rudzinski.

One of the most popular groups in Lake County is the Old-Fashioned Buckley Singers, three women who sing songs from American History, with special emphasis on the Civil War period. Photo by Patricia Young McKinlay.

chapter 8

Formal Learning

Most of the immigrants who made up Lake County's population before World War II were marginally educated with an abiding faith in education. Many were illiterate, even in their native languages, but they insisted that their offspring not be. No schools anywhere had fuller support of parents than those in Lake County. Good schools in Lake County were not just a collection of classrooms, they were shrines.

This partially explains why Gary spawned the nation's most famous education system in the first decade of the twentieth century. Dr. William A. Wirt's work-study-play method, aka platoon school, attracted so much attention and so many out-of-town visitors that a special office had to be established in Gary to deal with them. In all, more than two hundred school systems throughout the United States embraced all or parts of the Wirt system, and many of those schools still retain aspects of it.

Also in the first decade of the century, Edwin N. Canine installed a revolutionary educational system in East Chicago that took into account the city's almost total industrial environment, as well as its more than three-out-of-four foreign-born population. Long before there was such a thing as an intern-matching program, Canine matched students with jobs in local industry, the jobs becoming a goal for some and a way station for others. The power of the educational ideal caused East Chicago High School to invent and implement the state's first junior college in 1915.

Insistence that young people gain an education persists to this day. From the youngest pupil at a neighborhood elementary school to its scholars at nationally-recognized universities, Lake County sets high standards for education.

education

Lake County has a long history of producing its own professionals. The Cates twins, shown here after a trip to Ghana, plan to be physicians in related specialties and return to Gary to practice. *Times* photo by Tracy Albano.

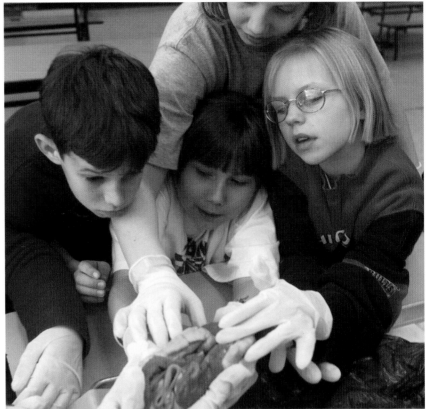

Whenever possible, Lake County schools tie into national programs that turn a spotlight on a particular issue, as is the case here at Munster's Elliott Elementary School. As part of the school's Heart Day activities, (left to right) Jordan Barnes, 10, Lindsey Pugh, 9, and Sar Schulte, 9, examine a cow's heart displayed by Indiana University Northwest medical student Mark McMurrey. *Times* photo by Tracy Albano.

Traditionally, Lake County schools do especially well in science competitions, which sometimes evoke the enthusiasm of sporting events. Here, in a moment of triumph, Lynn Podiecki rejoices with students at East Chicago's West Side Junior High School, which represented Northwest Indiana in the State Science Olympiad. *Times* photo by Zbigniew Bzak.

Natalie Biel, 17, front, gets into the performance with the Munster High School varsity pom pom team in the 1998 fifth annual Lake Central Dance Invitational. Times photo by Zbigniew Bzak.

Above: Lake County schools have pioneered in programs to help make students aware of differences in other students. Mickey Goodrich, special education teacher in Lake Station, is shown here helping Matthew Brant practice sign language, as part of a program to make students more aware and sensitive to diversity and disabilities. Times photo by Aldino Gallo.

Lake County schools have produced some of the nation's foremost leaders, and continue to do so. Alonzo Mendoza, Hammond High School 1998, shown here, represents the promise of another harvest of outstanding young people. PhotoCalumet image by Linda Dorman-Gainer.

Colleges Within Lake County

High school graduates have no need to stray far from home to find quality college education. Lake County campuses offer a mix of programs, from technical to professional. These campuses include those of Purdue University/Calumet (Hammond), Indiana University Northwest (Gary), Ivy Tech State College (East Chicago and Gary), Calumet College of Saint Joseph (Hammond), and Hyles-Anderson College (Crown Point).

Largest of Purdue University's regional campuses, Purdue University/Calumet offers degrees in more than eighty-five fields of study. In addition to bachelor's degrees, the college awards associate degrees on one end of the scale to master's degrees on the other. The school's co-op program with community businesses allows any of the more than nine thousand students to alternate semesters between working and taking full-time classes. The Hammond campus also has a well-respected engineering department, which has been recognized by *U.S. News & World Report* in its annual evaluation of colleges.

Moreover, PU/Cal offers elementary and high school students a unique educational opportunity through the Challenger Learning Center of Northwest Indiana. The program has been conceived to teach students the basics of science and mathematics through space flight simulations. During the simulations, students gain hands-on experience in spacecraft and Mission Control centers designed like the real thing. Located on the Woodmar (Hammond) campus, the $1.7 million center is one of only fifty such centers in North America, and serves students from three states.

Indiana University Northwest in Gary is the fourth-largest campus (of eight) of the Indiana University system. More than five thousand students are enrolled at this campus, which is set in thirty-three acres of Gary's two hundred forty acre Gleason Park. More than seventy degree programs are offered ranging from arts and sciences to business. IUN also houses the school of nursing plus a medical research center. The Center for Management Development in the School of Business provides comprehensive training services in ten categories of employment development and twelve categories of business consulting, including market study and analysis, total quality management, and performance-appraisal systems.

Two of Ivy Tech State College's instructional centers are located in Lake County, one in Gary, another in East Chicago. In addition to these campuses, each has a number of off-campus sites such as

Indiana University Northwest grew slowly from an extension of I.U. that conducted classes in high schools, to its own Calumet Center in East Chicago's Tod Park, to the present substantial campus in Gary's Gleason Park. Photo courtesy of Indiana University Northwest.

Calumet College began in East Chicago as an extension of St. Joseph and was a quick hit, gradually occupying about a dozen existing buildings. When Standard Oil (BP Amoco) moved its research staff to Naperville, Illinois, however, the school accepted the former research building, shown here, as a gift and transferred all East Chicago operations to Whiting/Robertsdale. Photo by Patricia Young McKinlay.

hospitals, businesses, and high schools. As Indiana's third largest state-supported institution, with twenty instructional centers throughout the state, Ivy Tech offers fifty career-oriented programs and majors in which students can earn a one-year certificate in a technical career field and/or a two-year associate's degree that is transferable to a four-year institution. Programs include business education, health- and human-services programs, and technical training. The Gary campus is home to an office of Business and Industry Training Programs that provides customized in-plant training for workforce development.

Calumet College of St. Joseph, located in Whiting/Robertsdale, was founded as an extension campus of St. Joseph's College. Today, the school is an independent liberal arts college devoted to serving non-traditional students, first-generation students (first in their family to attend college), and other minorities. The two hundred-sixty-acre campus is barrier-free to the handicapped. With courses offered on a flexible schedule, the twelve hundred students can pursue associate's or bachelor's degrees in a number of different majors. The school offers customized scheduling of day, evening, and weekend classes for students attempting to manage careers and families. The college operates a satellite campus in Merrillville, which is closer to where many students live or work.

Hyles-Anderson College in Crown Point is affiliated with the First Baptist Church of Hammond and stresses religious values.

Education in Lake County has become such big business that Purdue University/Calumet is now the second largest employer in the city of Hammond. Art by Alan Larkin.

Libraries

A sound community is a group of people surrounding a library.

Thus, the earliest-defined communities of Lake County revolved around libraries that were originally financed by the great steel magnate, Andrew Carnegie. Crown Point, Hammond, Whiting, East Chicago, Indiana Harbor, and Gary all had Carnegie libraries that evolved into systems. Some of the Lake County Carnegie libraries still stand, although greatly modernized; others have been replaced by new buildings and equipment. In communities where a free-standing city or town library could not be justified, the Lake County Library in Merrillville emerged to fill the void, operating as a first-class library in its own right, while providing services in support of smaller libraries.

Typical of the evolution of Lake County libraries is the one located in Hammond. When the Hammond Library came into existence in 1904, it immediately became one of the busiest institutions in the city. At first, the library was located in a corner of the

All of the major cities in Lake County once had Carnegie libraries. The oldest of these still standing is the Whiting Library, shown here, which was built in 1904. Photo by Patricia Young McKinlay.

138

Bloomhoff and Company Millinery Store. Later, it moved to the Chicago Telephone building on Rimbach Avenue. At that point, through the efforts of A. M. Turner, Dr. W. F. Howat, and other interested citizens, Andrew Carnegie was persuaded in contribute $27,000 to erect a new building.

With a promise from the city council that it would maintain a free public library, and with a gift of the lot for its location in Central Park, a new main building was opened to the public on July 8, 1905. In its first third of a century, 1904 to 1937, the Hammond library circulated almost five million volumes. At that point, the library consisted of its main building in Central Park plus six branches scattered throughout the city. Four of the branches were located in their own buildings, one in a bank building, and one in a settlement house.

During the Great Depression, circulation increased approximately two hundred percent, principally because of unemployment and the fact that people had more time to read, and found the library and its branches a haven for study. In deference to the city's ethnic make-up, the Hammond library of that time contained books in German, Polish, Slovakian, Bohemian, Hungarian, and Yiddish.

The second oldest Carnegie building is one in Crown Point that, with recent additions, is now called the Carnegie Center.
Photo by Patricia Young McKinlay.

As Lake County libraries developed, they sprouted specialized parts, the most popular of which have been historical collections, and in some cases facilities to house them. The Hammond Library, for example, has the Calumet Room; the Gary Library has the Indiana Room; and the East Chicago main library in Indiana Harbor has the East Chicago Room. Beyond municipal libraries, the libraries of colleges in Lake County also have historical collections, the largest and most comprehensive being the Indiana University Northwest Regional Archives.

Located on the third floor of the library at IUN, the Calumet Regional Archives was born in the early 1970s when James B. Lane and Ronald D. Cohen arrived at Indiana University Northwest to teach history. They quickly became interested in local history, but noted that some of it was being demolished in the civic insanity known as urban renewal. By moving fast, though, the two professors were able to rescue old documents from a settlement house that had a date with a steel ball. With that as a basis, the delving duo gathered other local historical papers and stored them in their offices, which became so crowded that each soon began to look like a dead letter office.

Museums

Visitors to Lake County often avail themselves of fascinating museums that tend to capture their attention and hold them until closing time. Most of the museums focus on a particular aspect of Lake County, as in the case of the Highland Museum, while others are all over the lot, as in the case of the Lake County Museum, located in the old courthouse building. Here are three more museums worth sampling:

The Dyer Historical Museum opened in the former Town Hall in 1975 in conjunction with America's Bicentennial. Except for such special occasions, however, most local artifacts have been kept in the homes of historical society members. That changed in 1988, when photos, clothing, household goods, and the like were moved to the new Town Hall, primarily for storage purposes. Until 1997, the museum more resembled a warehouse than a showplace. But that, too, changed.

The Hobart Historical Museum, dubbed the "town attic" because of its eclectic collection of artifacts, is Lake County's largest museum. Housed in an English Renaissance-style brick structure that was once the city library, the museum holds priceless treasures that date back centuries and give clues to the rich history of Hobart and Lake County.

The museum features a huge library of material that includes historic files on the United States, Indiana, and Lake County; local

Glen Eberly, president of the Dyer Historical Society, adds a record to the 1935 Wurlitzer jukebox saved from a bistro called Ma's Eats. The jukebox is on display at the Dyer Historical Museum, which preserves town artifacts. Times photo by Zbigniew Bzdak.

The historic bath house on Marquette Park Beach is in the process of being transformed into a museum that focuses on the birth of manned flight in the dunes. Photo by George Rogge.

newspapers, available on microfilm; a genealogy file of Hobart families; a federal census of Lake County; and an obituary file of Hobart families. There are also archives that include eight volumes of the adjutant Civil War general's reports of Indiana in the "War of the Rebellion."

The most user-friendly museum in Lake County is the one known as the Lake of the Red Cedars Museum, in Cedar Lake, which is a former boarding house that Armour Brothers built for its workers in 1895, when the company was harvesting ice from Cedar Lake. When ice harvesting declined with the rise of electrical refrigeration, the Lassen family acquired it, put runners on it, and, in 1919, slid it diagonally across Cedar Lake, where they used it as a hotel. In 1977, the town of Cedar Lake bought the building and leased it to the Cedar Lake Historical Association.

Built originally as a Carnegie library in 1914–15, this building was converted into the Hobart Historical Museum in 1968. It contains the greatest collection of historical artifacts and memorabilia in Lake County, as well as an extensive collection of historical books. Photo courtesy of the Hobart Historical Society.

The Association has cunningly used rooms on the first floor to depict the past: an old-fashioned Cedar Lake Hotel bar; a woman's boutique of 1870 onward; farm tool room; ice industry room; 1900s toy room; 1920s dining room; kitchen with wood-burning stove; parlor with victrola and old radio; general store; school room; physician's office; bedroom with soap stone bed warmers; a twenty-five-thousand-year-old mastodon bone and teeth and Indian artifacts. The museum is a history course in one afternoon.

Built in 1869, the Little Red School House in Hessville (Hammond) has been organized to celebrate the early teachers of Lake County and their methods and equipment. Photo by Richard Rudzinski.

Interstate Visitors Information Center

A singular, sculpted building of massive proportions, the new Lake County Interstate Visitors Information Center boldly captures the main images of the county. It tells the story of diversity and what is unique about Lake County, in addition to its people. Huge waves of stainless steel, signifying Lake Michigan, sweep onto the world famous Indiana sand dunes. Nudging the dunes is traditional industry, smoke stacks and a gray office building representing steel, still Lake County's major industry. Beyond industry lie plains and farms, fringed by the Kankakee River, Lake County's south border.

The building is the premier visitor information center in the Midwest. It helps promote awareness and appreciation of Lake County as well as its attractions, culture, and history.

Rather uniquely, the Center and all of the work of the Lake County Convention and Visitors Bureau costs the taxpayers of Lake County nothing. The Bureau's budget and operating expenses derive from part of the county's hotel/motel tax and from the riverboat gaming admission fee.

Externally, the unique design of the Lake County Interstate Visitors Information Center symbolically tells the story of the county. Internally, it houses functions of the Visitors Center. Photos on pages 142 and 143 courtesy of the Lake County Convention and Visitors Bureau.

Automobiles of various vintages are just one of the many displays staged in the Visitors Center. Indiana was one of the chief automobile centers of the world, with cars produced in both East Chicago and Gary.

The most distinctive structure of its type in Indiana, the Lake County Court House, shown here, is the fourth building so designated. The first was a log building erected in Liverpool, Lake County's first seat; when Crown Point was designated the county seat, however, the courthouse was rafted down the Little Calumet River to Blue Island, where it became a tavern. The second courthouse was a two-story log building, erected by Crown Point founder Solon Robinson and connected to a log store operated by him and his brother, Milo. The third building was a frame structure started in 1849 and designed by George Earl, founder of Lake Station, Liverpool, and Hobart.

Erected in 1849, this building lasted three decades until a robber, in a failed attempt to get his hands on $60,000 cash vaulted in the building to construct a new courthouse, blew up the frame building.

The nucleus of the present edifice was built in 1879. Compatible wings were added later until the present building evolved: a Victorian era structure that is a fascinating combination of Romanesque and Georgian styles. In 1907, Beers and Beers of Chicago designed two-story extensions, one for the north, the other for the south. Single-story wings were built in 1928.

Today, the evolved building houses the Lake County Historical Society, a historical museum, the Crown Point Chamber of Commerce, a photographic studio, a restaurant, and numerous boutiques. Most legal business is now conducted at the Lake County Government Center, a complex of buildings on the northside of Crown Point, completed in 1974.

The
JOHN DILLINGER
MUSEUM
A Hands-On Historical Adventure

A museum dedicated to the life and times of John Dillinger, the most pursued bank robber in American history, is a special part of the Visitors Center. Dillinger first gained national renown in 1934 when he robbed the First National Bank of East Chicago. His fame gained mythic proportions when, later that year, he broke out of the supposedly escape-proof Crown Point Jail.

The Dillinger Museum includes a reproduction of the spot in Chicago where John Dillinger was gunned down by East Chicago police and FBI agents.

chapter 9

The sweep of Lake County's municipal personalities is truly breathtaking, a thrilling diapason of moods and emotions. From the sea-like Lake Michigan and its glories to the northern tier where brutal mills have hammered their communities into tough towns to farmland centers where Grant Wood would never have had to move his easel to river country where the chief exertion is digging for worms, Lake County has it all.

Let us pause briefly, therefore, to consider the major communities of Lake County.

Steel Coast
Hammond

The second largest city in Lake County is in the process of reinventing itself, in significant part around the new federal courthouse shown here in the early stages of construction. It is not the city's first reinvention. In 1901 its seminal industry, the George H. Hammond Packing Company (built in 1869), burned to the ground and the city miraculously came back with a highly diversified metropolis of a hundred seventy-five industries and, ultimately, a population of more than 175,000 at its peak, some living in the finest homes in Lake County. By then a complex commercial hub, Hammond drew patrons from the entire county. With the end of the Industrial Age, the dawn of the Information Age, and the population shift southward, Hammond's population plummeted, according to the 1990 census, to 84,236, as the commercial concentration moved across the state line to River Oaks regional shopping center in Calumet City. Today, Hammond is gradually becoming a services center that includes, in addition to the new federal courthouse, an eye-popping Visitors and Convention Bureau building, the Empress Casino in Robertsdale, and a number of computer-driven businesses. And more are on the way. Times *photo by Tracy Albano.*

Facing page: Art by Fred Semmler.

146

community glimpses

AMERICA'S CROSSROADS
in Northwest Indiana, where the highway
structure easily allows the world to pass through
or stop to enjoy the beautiful environment
along the SOUTH SHORE LINE

Whiting/Robertsdale

Whiting, including Robertsdale which is legally part of Hammond, has aptly been dubbed the Mayberry R.F.D. of Lake County. It has changed less than any city in the county. Community gatherings such as the one shown here downtown, are as common as pierogi, if not blueberry pie. The main drag, 119th Street, still features non-mall shops and human beings who actually walk up and down the street. The community features two of the finest restaurants in Lake County, Phil Smidt's and Keith's, and one of the most comfortable family restaurants, Up for Grabs. Carolers stroll throughout the town during Christmas season, and the community annually puts on a concert by Chorus Angelorum, one of the finest singing groups in Greater Chicago. Despite the downsizing of the Standard Oil (BP Amoco) refinery, built in 1889 and once called the largest complete refinery in the world, the population hardly ever changes. Houses are in such hot demand that they tend to be handed down from generation to generation. Whiting's classic Carnegie Library (1903) is one of the most user-friendly in the county, and local schools have maintained a high level of quality for more than a century. The Lake Michigan beach attracts thousands in the summer, and Wolf Lake has been rated one of the finest wind surfing bodies of water in the nation. In the winter, the Community House provides multiple activities. No city in Lake County provides a higher quality of life. *Photo courtesy of the Whiting Chamber of Commerce.*

East Chicago

The municipality of East Chicago is confusingly both the whole and the part, which is why it is known as the Twin City. East Chicago the part is on the west side of the Indiana Harbor Ship Canal, which splits the municipality. After a long argument about location, the city hall shown here, was built in East Chicago in 1908, with Indiana Harbor receiving a lakefront park. East Chicago was laid out and built up in 1888, with industry hugging the banks of the canal and a parallel belt railroad. The name was chosen to give European investors the impression that it was part of Chicago, where a boom was in progress. East Chicago began auspiciously, with such major factories as the William Graver Tank Works (the town's first industry), Famous Manufacturing Company, C. A. Treat Car Wheel Works, Chicago Horseshoe Factory, the National Forge and Iron Company, and others built in the first five years, or until the Panic of 1893 froze construction. Historically, the community comprised four quadrants, each with its own ethnic make-up: predominantly Welsh and Irish in the northwest, Polish in the southwest, Italian in the southeast, and a miscellany in the northeast. Outside of Lake County, East Chicago is best known for its championship high school football teams, co-coached by Pete Ruzinski and Ernie Miller. E. C. Roosevelt compiled a record unmatched by any team in Indiana, winning or sharing the state championship eight times, going undefeated six times, and once winning thirty-four consecutive games. E. C. Roosevelt also won a state basketball championship in 1970. *Photo by Richard D. Rudzinski.*

Indiana Harbor

The ultimate melting pot of America (thanks to industrial recruiters), Indiana Harbor once contained more than a hundred different races and nationalities. Most had their own celebrations, such as the parade shown here to praise Puerto Rico. Although always part of East Chicago politically, Indiana Harbor came into existence thirteen years after its fraternal twin, with the building of Inland Steel and other heavy industry along the Indiana Harbor Ship Canal. Because of the canal, vast switching yards, and poor roads, Indiana Harbor developed separately, with its own business, manufacturing, and residential districts, while its chauvinistic thought and action often resulted in sectional strife in municipal affairs. On the eve of the Information Age,

Inland was the largest single steel plant in the nation, and Indiana Harbor was probably the most industrialized piece of real estate in the world. As a project of the Lake Michigan Land Company, the community sprang (1901–04) up like a Hollywood set. Within three years, the Lake Michigan Land Company had leveled sand ridges; laid out streets; installed sewers; hooked into existing water, electric, and gas systems; built six hundred houses and stores as well as the finest hotel south of Hyde Park; caused a school to be built; influenced the transportation service into and out of town; provided electric lights and gas; built many miles of boardwalks; paved a few macadam streets and cement sidewalks; planted five thousand shade trees; reserved land for a lakefront public park and another park south of 141st Street; dedicated a strip of land for houses fronting the lake; and generally created a boom town. In 1904, the new industrial city of Indiana Harbor was a reality, billed as "The Twentieth Center Wonder," just nineteen miles southeast of downtown Chicago. In 1960, Indiana Harbor produced Lake County's second state championship basketball team, E. C. Washington winning again in 1971 with "the greatest high school team ever." Today the community boasts Pastrick Marina and harbors Harrah's East Chicago, the largest casino boat on Lake Michigan. *Photo by Patricia Young McKinlay.*

Buffington Harbor

Known far and wide today as the home of two casino boats, the Majestic Star and Trump's Casino and Hotel, Buffington Harbor was once the deepest and largest private harbor on Lake Michigan, extending out to the lighthouse shown here. Buffington began as Edgemoor, an enclave of Irish railroad workers, who, using a handcart, attended church in Whiting and buried their dead in Chesterton. In 1903, Illinois Steel (of South Chicago) established its cement plant at Edgemoor, whose name was changed to Buffington, in honor of E. J. Buffington, the company's president. Buffington immediately became the major cement supplier for the Panama Canal, which was then under construction. When the deep harbor was finally built more than two decades later, U.S. Vice President Charles C. Dawes appeared to dedicate it. From that point on (1927), a new era in the movement of cement from Lake County began and the Universal Portland Cement Company (later known as Universal Atlas) went on to become the largest producer of cement in the world. Although located within the city limits of Gary, virtually all of the cement plant workers, including management, lived in Indiana Harbor and walked to work. Today, it is possible to walk from Harrah's East Chicago to Buffington Majestic Star and Trump Casino in less than half an hour, although most people rely on wheels. *Photo by Patricia Young McKinlay.*

Gary

No city in Lake County has attracted so much national attention as Gary, the self-described "City of the Century," aka "The Magic City." Although the youngest of cities in Lake County, Gary became the largest, at one time flirting with a population of 200,000. Its preeminence is symbolized by its front yard, Gateway Park, which features adjacent to it twin municipal and county buildings, shown here, the former dedicated in 1928, the latter in 1929. The city's cre-

ation was a product of the newly-amalgamated U.S. Steel Corporation's decision to build a totally-integrated steel mill (Indiana Steel Company) in the dunes country, and an ideal city to go with the mills. For many years, Gary was virtually a one-industry city and, as such, received a good deal of attention in national media. It was also a city whose north-south spine became a major commercial focus, whose utilities were first-rate, whose many institutions grew strong, and whose fire and police departments were first-rate. It was also a divided city, however, with management and skilled workers living north of the Wabash tracks, and everyone else south of the tracks, the yeastiest community being The Patch, later known as the Central District. Despite such divisions, the most discussed and debated feature of Gary was its extraordinarily innovative school system, designed by Dr. William A. Wirt, its creator and manager for about a third of a century. Emulated throughout the world, the Gary system shaped more than two hundred school systems in the U.S., which copied or adapted it. In the late 1960s, however, Gary all but collapsed and tens of thousands of people fled, inspiring such mocking bumper strips, as: "The last one out of Gary, please turn out the lights." But all of that changed with the new millennium. After scraping the bottom of the rust bowl in the late-twentieth century, Gary entered 2000 A.D. with the determination of a phoenix. Pan American Airlines began daily flights to Orlando, Pittsburgh, and Boston (Portsmouth, N.H.); the city signed a deal to bring a Continental Basketball Association team (the Steelheads) to Gary; the city entered a contract to host the nationally-televised Miss USA Pageant, starting in 2001; the city also conducted negotiations to bring a minor league baseball team to Gary in 2002; city officials sought to convert three downtown buildings into an indoor/outdoor theater; the majestic City Methodist Church, a de facto civic center, is being converted into a cultural center; a new or renovated hotel is being pursued; Gary's Union Station on the side of the Indiana Tollway may be converted into a visitors' center; public housing is being torn down and rebuilt; a former Naval Reserve property on Lake Michigan (Miller Beach) may be transformed into a gated community of upscale housing; and one of the casinos has already built a hotel and the other is developing property to include another hotel, marina, parking garages, shops, and recreation. *Photo by Richard D. Rudzinski.*

Miller Beach

Miller Beach

Gary coveted Miller Beach from the start, even trying to annex it in 1906, the year Gary began. At the time, Miller Beach was the major fishing station of Lake County. It was not until 1919, however, that the deed was done, when U.S. Steel bought one hundred twenty acres on Miller's lakefront and donated the land to the city of Gary as a park, even as Gary annexed the land and the village of Miller. The park was known as Lake Front Park until 1930, when the name was changed to Marquette Park, in honor of Father Jacques Marquette, who camped there just before he died in Michigan. In 1922, Gary built an elaborate bath-house, now called the Aquatorium, and a year later, it built what came to be known as Marquette Park Pavilion, with dancing indoors and outdoors on a terrace that had steps leading into the Marquette Park lagoon, shown here. Miller Beach was also the site of two major international events. In 1896, Octave Chanute conducted his history-making glider experiments in Miller, which led to the fuselage of the Wright brothers' flying machine. That same year, Professor Henry Chandler Cowles practically invented the science of ecology in the dunes of Miller and to the east. For all of the twentieth century, the beaches of Miller have been the most heavily used in Lake County. *Photo courtesy of the Gary Chamber of Commerce.*

The Ridge
Munster

Growing slowly and steadily for more than a century and a half, the Dutch community of Munster has evolved into one of the

blue-chip cities of Indiana, with the state's highest per capita income, the second best education system, a 500-physician hospital, a multi-faceted arts center, booming light industry, and a variety of fine specialty services. It all began with the property shown here. In 1837, David Gibson built an inn on the corner of what is today Columbia Avenue and Ridge Road, an old stagecoach trail. In 1845, Allen and Julia Watkins Brass took over the property and enlarged it into the Brass Tavern, with two downstairs parlors and six upstairs rooms. In 1864, the Brasses sold the inn to Johann and Wilhelmina Stallbohm who renamed it the Stallbohm Inn. When the Stallbohms installed a telegraph, the inn became the national news center of Lake County. The Stallbohms closed the inn in the 1890s; their daughter and son-in-law, Wilhelmina and Hugo Kaske, lived in the building. Alas, in 1909, after a Halloween party, the old inn burned to the ground, although the barn shown here was spared. In 1910, the neighboring Kooy brothers rebuilt the house, farther from Ridge Road than the original. In 1968, the Munster Park Board bought the house and surrounding land and turned the site into Heritage Park. *Photo by Patricia Young McKinlay.*

Highland

Lake County overflows with patriotic expression, as exemplified here by Highland's Monument of Flags, which is aptly located across the street from Wicker Memorial Park, a living monument to World War I fallen soldiers who sought to make the world safe for democracy. The park was dedicated on Flag Day, 1927, by President Calvin Coolidge. A 453-acre township facility, Wicker Memorial Park comprises an 18-hole golf course, driving range, swimming pool, lighted tennis courts, wintertime ice skating, sand volleyball courts, and areas with shelters for family and group picnics. Centerpiece of the park is a million-dollar social center overlooking a man-made lake,  which has a banquet room that seats five hundred and can be reserved for weddings and other special events. Highland's first settlers were Michael and Judy Johnston in 1847, who were quickly followed by first German and then Dutch immigrants, who drained the swampy land and raised vegetables, notably cabbages for the settlement's first industry, a sauerkraut factory. When the first five blocks of Highland were platted in 1882, the settlement was called Clough Postal Station, a name that a year later gave way to Highlands (plural), a descriptive name because it was located high on Calumet Beach, a glacier residue. Today, Highland can be described as a mature suburb of 25,000 people with excellent housing in quiet neighborhoods, lush parks, fine schools and teachers, extensive shopping facilities, and a location convenient to both the mills of north county and the diversions of Chicago. *Photo by Paul A. Meyers.*

Griffith

Griffith today has a highly enlightened educational system, as can be seen here as Jessica Koch, 9, (left) and Bridgett Vechey, 9, learn about sign language at the Ready Elementary School. But the town owes its existence to railroads. First settled in 1853 by Mathias and Anna Miller who produced eight children there, Griffith took shape as a town when it became a crossroads of several railroads: the Erie Kalamazoo (Michigan Central) in 1852, a branch (from Joliet) of the Michigan Southern in 1854, plus the Elgin, Joliet and Eastern, the Grand Trunk, and the Chicago and Erie. (Four railroads crossed at what became the center of town.) As the gangs of high ballers and gandy dancers pushed the steel ribbon forward, many of the workers saw the opportunities offered in Griffith and settled down to farm, at least part time. Others supplied the railroads with provisions, such as wood and produce. As the railroads expanded, they brought more residents, who built homes there near their railroad jobs, while maintaining farms on the outskirts of the town area. After several false starts, Griffith began to come into its own following World War II, when the population of Lake County began to shift southward from the industrial north. Today, it is a mature suburb of pleasant neighborhoods and solid citizens, whose bounds also include Hoosier Prairie and Oak Ridge Prairie County Park. Times *photo by Zbigniew Bzdak.*

Lake Station

Lake Station is a blue collar bedroom community that is full of surprises, like the St. Francis Xavier shrine shown here that was

designed and built by Edward P. Kipta, a one-time Frank Lloyd Wright apprentice and supervisor. The town dates from 1836 when George Earle, an artist and architect from England, bought the paper city of Liverpool, now subsumed in Lake Station, which he steered into becoming Lake County's first seat. After the county seat removed to Crown Point, Lake Station became the principal shipping point in Lake County, mainly because it became, in 1851, the western terminus of the Michigan Central Railroad. Farmers shipped their produce from that point and passengers transferred from rail to stagecoach, often staying at the Audubon Hotel. One of those passengers was Abraham Lincoln, who was enroute to the first Republican convention in Jackson, Michigan. The town gained a sudden surge of interest in 1908, when William Earle, son of George, founded and platted the new suburb of East Gary, intending that it be a white collar suburb for the officers, department heads, executives, and professional workers of the new steel mill that U.S. Steel had begun to build in 1906. More than a half-century later, the town reverted to its original name and Lake Station continues to be a solid and interesting community. *Photo by Patricia Young McKinlay.*

Hobart

The All American community of Hobart could be the set for everything Americana, such as its well-known doughboy statue shown here. Its founder, however, was an Englishman. In 1847, George Earle moved his family from Liverpool into a log house in Hobart, and since he was the postmaster, the post office also moved to Hobart. In 1849, George Earle platted the new town, quickly building a gristmill and damming Deep River to create Lake George, around which a model community grew up. Hobart's main claim to industrial fame became brickmaking. It began in 1872 after James Guyer established a brickyard near Ridge Road and Lake Park Avenue; the yard eventually produced some 800,000 bricks a year. Other brickyards followed suit. At the turn of the century, the Waterbury yard produced about 1.5 billion common and pressed-brick annually. All yards relied on a presumably inexhaustible supply of fine blue clay found eighty feet below the ground surface. From the start, Hobart as a town and city was well managed, having a good water supply, electric power facility, telephone office, and other infrastructure. Hobart also adapted intelligently to external conditions, such as the post–World War II housing boom, without losing its distinctive social and cultural qualities. In recent time, Hobart gained celebrity as the home of high school football powers, its teams winning state championships in 1987, 1989, 1991, and 1993. From an early date, the community gained national attention with its high school bands, which often were the best in the land. And Pavel Farms in Hobart became the largest breeder of Arabian horses in the state of Indiana. *Photo courtesy of the Hobart Chamber of Commerce.*

The Midlands

Dyer

Dyer gained national attention and lasting influence when, in 1921, a three-mile experimental highway was laid. It was known as The Ideal Section of the Lincoln Highway. The Section tested many innovations used even today on the nation's Interstate system. Shown here is Bruno Dravininkas marking the station number at the west end of the Ideal Section, when modernization began in 1997. The Lincoln Highway through Dyer was originally part of an Indian trail used for travel from Nebraska to Canada. With settlement, it became a stagecoach route that produced, in 1838, a tavern (food and lodging) known as the State Line House, aka Half-Way House, on the southeast corner of U.S. 30 and Hart Street. The Michigan Central Railroad and the Joliet Cut-Off gave Dyer the distinction of being one of the first three rail stations in Northwest Indiana. The Michigan Central also built a grain elevator, which attracted farmers from thirty miles away. Aaron Hart, who owned 20,000 acres in the vicinity, platted Dyer in 1858, and the town soon exceeded Lake Station in shipping agricultural products. Dyer was also renowned for the livestock raised by Englishman George F. Davis, who was most famous for developing a new breed of swine, the Victoria, which won blue ribbons at fairs everywhere. Today, Dyer is a decidedly upscale suburb whose points of interest include Meyer Castle and part of Briar Ridge, a community-within-a-community that is built around a golf course and features million-dollar homes. *Photo by Art Schweitzer.*

Schererville

In recent years, no part of Lake County has experienced the growth of Schererville, a delightful community of modern homes especially favored by refugees from Illinois. Although there had

been settlers in the neighborhood for a number of years, Schererville really began in 1865, when Nicholas Scherer bought land from Aaron Hart and laid out the town. At the time, Schererville consisted of about twenty-five families, most of whom were German Catholics, as were most of the people in St. John Township. Apart from religion, a major passion of the denizens was education, as symbolized by the horse-drawn school bus here, which operated well into the twentieth century. Even before Scherer platted his town, Aaron Hart, who drained thousands of acres of swamp in the vicinity, moved his family in 1861 to Hartsdale Farm, an 8,000-acre farm that was a model farm. Eventually, Hartsdale Farm was crossed by five railroads. Schererville, however, remained small for most of a century, known mainly at first for Teibel's restaurant, established in 1929, and later for Hoosier Boys' Town, the Scherwood Club (golf, food), and the Illiana Motor Speedway. But in the late–twentieth century, Schererville suddenly mushroomed, becoming so popular that a Chicago publication called it the hottest town in Greater Chicago. The town of Schererville is aptly-named "Crossroads of America," because the intersection of U.S. 41 and U.S. 30, historically had been a crossing of many Indian trails. *Photo courtesy of Art Schweitzer.*

Merrillville

Following the building, in the mid–1960s, of I-65 and the Twin Towers office complex, shown here, at the intersection of U.S. 30 and I-65, Merrillville became Lake County's commercial hub, a place where people never run out of things to do. In 1834, Merrillville was a prairie surrounded by woods when Jeremiah Wiggins, the first settler, stopped his covered wagon at McGwinn's Village to water his horses. McGwinn's Village featured a huge dancing floor and the largest Indian cemetery in Lake County. There Wiggins staked his claim, creating Wiggins' Point, the original name of Merrillville. Other settlers followed and, during the Gold Rush of 1849, the California Exchange Hotel sprang up on the Sauk Trail (approximately U.S. 30), a main route to the West. What became Merrillville grew slowly for more than a century until the late 1960s, when a flood of people from Gary rolled southward to take up new ground. The result has been phenomenal. The erstwhile lazy country town now boasts: many fine hotels/motels, a show stage sought out by entertainment greats, a place kids can call their own (Celebration Station), one hundred thirty restaurants, fests and parades galore, stunning Old World church buildings, more than five hundred stores in which to shop, golf courses, a planetarium, a swimming pool, Deep River County Park, a huge high school football stadium, the main Lake County Public Library, art galleries, fashion boutiques, discount shops, movies, a beach at Hidden Lake, fitness centers, U-pick farms, modern homes, a church for every belief, a retirement community, an off track betting parlor, a water park, and just about anything that can be found in a large metropolis. *Photo courtesy of NIPSCO.*

St. John

In the last three decades of the twentieth century, St. John has become one of the most desirable places to live in Lake County.

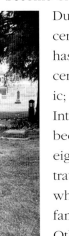

During the 1970s alone, population exploded by 126 percent, and is still growing, while an infrastructure program has taken on a frenzied aspect. By 1980, according to the census, St. John's people had become well-to-do and prolific; only Munster had a higher median household income. Interestingly, St. John's per capita income was not higher because 36.6 percent of the 1980 population was under eighteen years of age, St. John's having the highest concentration of young people in Lake County. St. John began when John Hack, a German immigrant, arrived with his family in 1837 in what was then known as Western Prairie.

Other land-hungry Germans soon followed and a community formed. Soon, Hack, a religious man, erected a crude frame church on his property, with everything being hauled from Chicago by teams of oxen, each trip requiring a week. The resulting structure was the first Catholic church in Lake County, and became known as the mother church of others that followed. The historic log church, shown here, now located on the present church grounds, became the second Catholic church in St. John, after the home of John Hack. The town really began to grow when what is now U.S. 41 evolved from a mud road to a cinder road and finally to a modern concrete highway. As late as the 1920s, farmers had difficulty negotiating mud roads in automobiles: One farmer even used a team of horses to pull his automobile to St. John, where U.S. 41 was packed with cinders. At that point he would unhitch the team, tie them to a hitching post, and drive his auto the rest of the way into town. *Photo by Patricia Young McKinlay.*

Crown Point

Crown Point distills the essence of every county seat in Indiana, and harbors memories so distinctly its own that the city has a special place in Americana. Founded in 1834 by Solon Robinson, the town built up around a county courthouse, part of which is shown here. Indeed, the courthouse is the most distinctive one in the state. Despite its relative antiquity, Crown Point is one of the fastest-growing cities of Lake County and contains some of its finest houses and apartments. Its historic homes constitute a two-mile, self-guided tour that begins on the town square and exposes much of the history of Lake County. Until late in the 1930s, Crown Point was known as the Gretna Green of America, where marriage mills cranked out hitched couples around the clock. In 1934, Crown Point also became part of American legend when John Dillinger broke out of a so-called escape-proof jail and generated national headlines for several months thereafter. In 1909, it was central to the Cobe Cup race, a precursor of the Indianapolis 500. More recently, it was the home of Jerry Ross, the astronaut who has spent more time in space than any other mortal. Crown Point is also home to the Lake County Fairgrounds, one of the most popular retreats in the county, especially during the County Fair in late August. The mural in the Crown Point post office is a fine example of the 1930s WPA program for artists and writers. When tuberculosis was ravaging the land, the Parramore Sanitarium was built in Crown Point, one of the finest facilities of its kind in the nation. On the political front, Barlett Woods helped organize the Free Soil Party, an anti-slavery third party that some people feel evolved into the Republican Party. All of these things and much more are displayed in the Court House Museum in the Old Courthouse, which is open to the public every Friday, Saturday, and Sunday afternoons. *Photo courtesy of Lake County Visitors and Convention Bureau.*

Cedar Lake

Cedar Lake is a body of water, a town, and a composite of communities, some long gone or absorbed, towns like Armour, Paisley, and others. In the early twentieth century, the lake fringe was the only industrial area in Lake County, an area that could boast ice industries, a bell factory, a handle factory, and a booming tourist and hotel industry. In 1892, Cedar Lake became a summer resort and, until World War II, was one of Indiana's most famous resorts. It housed visitors in forty-seven separate hotels, and the area was renowned for swimming, productive fishing, golfing, and sailing, such as the Cedar Lake regatta, shown here. It was the training ground for such celebrities as Jack Johnson, the heavyweight champion of the world, and Johnny Weismuller, Tarzan of the movies. As IUN Professor James B. Lane has written, "The place also inspired poets and songwriters, inventors and impresarios, racketeers and robber barons, socialites and comedians, including such notables as foot specialist Dr. Scholl . . .

evangelist Dwight Moody . . .," and others. But during the war, when thousands of workers from various parts of the U.S. converged on the mills of Lake County, many of the newcomers seeking housing occupied cottages on tiny lots in Cedar Lake, and the result was an ecological disaster that just about killed the lake. Since the 1960s, Cedar Lake has been making a comeback, although Lane calls it "a town in flux socially, culturally, politically, and economically, meanwhile searching for a modern identity." But it still has an asset that no other inland community in Lake County has: the spring-fed lake Indians called Mus-qua-ack-ack-bis, and which the first county surveyors called Clear Lake. Times *photo by John J. Watkins.*

Tri Creek
Lowell

Lowell, the capital of Lake County's farm country, is the last of the cities in Lake County to retain a rural, small-town atmosphere, as symbolized by the silo shown here. This is an irresistible appeal to urbanites and suburbanites bent on becoming ex-urbanites, which explains why the town's population increased from 3,839 in 1970 to 5,827 in 1980 to 6,430 in 1990. It may also explain why such a comparatively small town has a dozen antique shops. After a few settlers arrived in the Lowell, Creston, Shelby, and contiguous areas, Melvin A. Halstead came in 1845 at the age of 24, established a sawmill and brick factory, and built a home of 400,000 bricks. After seeking his fortune in California during the Gold Rush, he returned in 1852 and, within a year, built a flour mill, laid out lots, and established the town of Lowell. In later years he built a two-story brick schoolhouse, then the largest in Lake County, and a three-story brick factory building. He also brought to Lowell, in 1880, its first railroad, the Monon. Today, Lowell has become a prestigious executive community, while still retaining its rural character. Its Labor Day Parade is the oldest in Indiana. Among celebrities produced in Lowell and vicinity are Bobo Rockefeller, former wife of Arkansas governor Winthrop Rockefeller and mother of Winnie; and Jo Anne Worley, an actress with a book full of credits but best known for her role in the 1960s television series, "Laugh In." *Photo by Larry Brechner.*

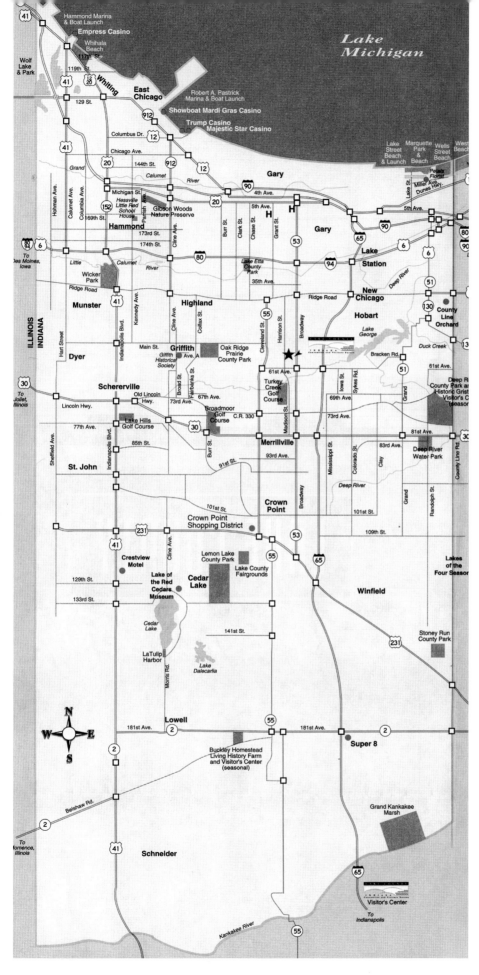

Lake County can be divided into four zones, each with its own character within an overall county character. The Steel Coast on Lake Michigan includes the municipalities of Whiting, Hammond, East Chicago, and Gary. The Ridge includes Munster, Highland, Griffith, Hobart, and Lake Station. The Midlands include Dyer, Schererville, Merrillville, Crown Point, and Cedar Lake. Tri Creek includes Lowell and towns located in what was once the Great Kankakee Marsh, including Schneider and Shelby.

Map courtesy of the Lake County Convention and Visitors Bureau.

chapter 10

The only true measure of a place is the kind of people it produces. For some reason too complex to explain here, Lake County produces not only solid citizens who contribute to the development of their respective communities, but a disproportionate number who go on to attain the highest laurels of their profession, and to other achievements. Here are just a few who made it to the very top.

Nobel Prize

Dr. Ferid Murad of Whiting won a 1998 Nobel Prize in medicine. His work led to treating disorders ranging from heart disease to shock, and also led to the development of pharmaceuticals for the treatment of impotence. In 1970, Dr. Paul Samuelson of Gary won the Nobel Prize for economics. *Photo courtesy of the Whiting Chamber of Commerce.*

Virtuoso

Pianist Irene Levy Alexander of Indiana Harbor began playing concerts and recitals as a child prodigy and is still going strong as an octogenarian. Since she debuted at New York's Town Hall, she has played at numerous stateside venues, from Chicago's Orchestra Hall to both coasts, and internationally from Israel to China. Presently, she plays more than one hundred fifty mini-concerts a year, and, during the next two years, plans to perform concerts in every state of the union, as well as eight nations in Europe. *Maurice Seymour photo.*

laureates

Academy Award

Karl Malden, nee Mladen Sekulovich of Gary, won an Oscar in 1951 for his role as Blanche's suitor in "A Streetcar Named Desire." He was nominated again for his role as a priest in "On the Waterfront," starring Marlon Brando, and also appeared in dozens of memorable films, including "Birdman of Alcatraz," "Gypsy," "The Cincinnati Kid," "Baby Doll," and "Patton," the last named also featuring Hammond's James Edwards as Patton's aide. Malden performed in many television plays, including the series "The Streets of San Francisco," co-starring Michael Douglas who played Malden's young partner. Not only did Karl Malden win an Oscar, he also won a TV Emmy for the mini-series "Fatal Vision." In his well-received but short-lived series "Skag," Malden played a Serbian steelworker, which, he said, "did an awful lot for me emotionally, enabling me to pay something back to my heritage." Malden is shown here with his father, Peter, a real life Skag, during Gary's Jubilee in 1956. A generation later, another Serb, Steve Tesich of East Chicago, also won an Oscar for writing the script for "Breaking Away." *Photo courtesy of the Calumet Regional Archives of Indiana University Northwest.*

Emmy and Peabody

Frank Reynolds of East Chicago and Indiana Harbor anchored ABC's Emmy-winning coverage of President Nixon's visit to China, and in 1980 won another Emmy for his reporting on ABC News' post–election special edition. He also won the George Foster Peabody Award, broadcasting's highest honor, for his defense of the press against former Vice President Spiro Agnew. Hammond's Jules Power, writer/director/producer of many TV shows, also won the Peabody and several Emmys. *Photo courtesy of the Calumet Regional Archives of Indiana University Northwest.*

Emmy

John Chulay, shown here on the right, was assistant director and director of both the Dick Van Dyke Show and the Mary Tyler Moore Show, both of which won multiple Emmys. To his left is his sister, actress Marian Collier, co-star of the TV series Mr. Novak, who acted in many TV shows and motion pictures. Natives of Indiana Harbor, John and Marian are shown here in Germany on the set of "Inside the Third Reich," a 1981 ABC-TV mini-series. *Photo courtesy of Violet Manuszak.*

Grammy

For most of three decades, Michael Jackson of Gary won Grammys as often as ordinary people win prizes in Crackerjack boxes. There had never been anyone like him in show business history. He is shown here in 1975 with his brothers ("The Jackson 5") and publisher J. T. Harris during a visit to Gary. Left to right: Tito, Jermaine, Jackie, Marlon, Michael, and Randy. *Photo courtesy of the Calumet Regional Archives of Indiana University Northwest.*

World's Champion

Known as the "Man of Steel," Tony Zale (nee Zaleski) of Gary won the National Boxing Association middleweight title in 1941. After spending World War II in the Navy, Zale fought arguably the three most memorable fights in boxing history with Rocky Grazianao, winning the first, losing the second, and winning the third. He retired in 1949 after losing to Marcel Cerdan of France. *Photo courtesy of the Calumet Regional Archives of Indiana University Northwest.*

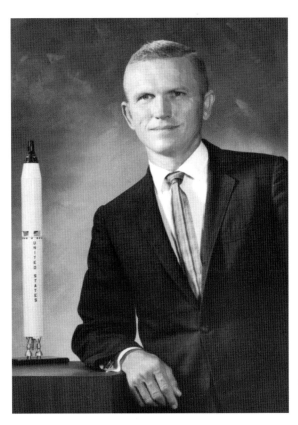

First to the Moon

On Christmas Eve, 1968, Gary's Colonel Frank Borman flew around the moon with his crew of Major William A. Anders and Captain James A. Lovell, Jr. It was the most far-reaching voyage of the space age to that date. After the astronauts flew twice around the moon in egg-shaped orbits, they dropped to a circular orbit nearly seventy miles above the dusty craters, plains, and mountains of the lunar surface. Colonel Borman described the moon as a "vast, lonely, and forbidding sight," adding that it was "not a very inviting place to live or work," which was a withering indictment coming from someone who grew up in sooty Gary before recent pure air initiatives. In later years, Colonel Jerry L. Ross of Crown Point spent more time in space than anyone, and was part of a crew that worked to assemble an International Space Station. *Photo courtesy of the Calumet Regional Archives of Indiana University Northwest.*

World's Top Masters

Jim Platis, left, named the world's top track athlete in his age category, won six gold medals at the Senior Olympics in Madrid, Spain, in 1992, five more golds at the Senior Olympics held in Atlanta in 1996, and seven golds at the games in Australia in 2000. In the process, he set world's records in the 100- and 200-meter dashes, as well as the long jump, triple jump, and high jump. His wife, Mary Lou, right, who once ranked second in the nation in her age group, specializes in field events. *Photo by Richard D. Rudzinski.*

Scoring Champ

Kristina Divjak, a six-foot forward at North-western University, led the Big Ten in scoring. She ranked among the top twenty-five players in the nation in three statistical categories: scoring, three-pointers, and free thrown percentage. At Lake Central High School in St. John, she led her team to the 1994 state championship, following in the footsteps of her father, who captained Washington High School of Indiana Harbor to a state championship in 1960. After posting a 4.5 grade point average in high school, she planned her education so that she could become a physician. In 1998, Kristina was chosen one of the ten most influential women in Lake County. Times *photo by Tracy Albano.*

Top of the Charts

When four mop-haired Liverpudlians achieved an unprecedented level of entertainment success, it was Gary's Vivian Carter who gave them access to American turntables through her Vee-Jay record label. A female Horatio Alger, Vivian, operating out of a record shop at an old dry cleaning store in Gary, ran $300 into an empire. In 1964, four of the nation's top ten records wore Vee-Jay labels. She also pioneered crossover music, which allowed African-American rhythm and blues music to reach the general population. *Photo courtesy of the Calumet Regional Archives of Indiana University Northwest.*

World's Junior Champion

Mary Lou Piatek-Daniels of Whiting and Munster became the world's Number One women's junior tennis player in 1979. She turned professional in 1980 and toured for fifteen years, being ranked fifteenth in the world in 1982–83. A fixture at Wimbledon for thirteen years, she once played Chris Everett at Center Court of Wimbledon. After retiring from the tour, she continues to play four days a week and also participates in events organized by Grand Slam Sports of North Miami Beach. *Photo courtesy of the Calumet Regional Archives of Indiana University Northwest.*

Most Successful Woman

Mildred Carlson (Ahlgren) of Indiana Harbor and Whiting was named one of the six most successful women in America in 1953 by the *Women's Home Companion* magazine. This designation derived from twenty years of urging women to play an active role in public affairs, and from the fact that she was president of the 11,000,000-member General Federation of Women's Clubs. *Associated Press Photo.*

Heisman Trophy Winner

At Gary Horace Mann High School, Tom Harmon led the Horsemen to an undefeated season while scoring 150 points and being named the best quarterback in the state. He also captained the Horace Mann basketball team, pitched three no-hitters for the baseball team, and set a state track record for the 200-yard low hurdles. At the University of Michigan, he was an All-American in both 1939 and 1940 and capped off a college career in which he was often compared favorably with Red Grange by winning the coveted Heisman Trophy as the best player in America. He served as an Air Force pilot in World War II. His son, Mark Harmon, is an actor who stars on "Chicago Hope." *Photo courtesy of the Calumet Regional Archives of Indiana University Northwest.*

Super Bowl Champ

In 1970, Gary's "Hurrying Henry" Stram coached the Kansas City Chiefs to the National Football League championship, after reaching the Super Bowl in 1966. In all, Hank Stram's teams won five NFL inter-divisional and divisional playoffs. Four times "coach of the year," he coached two Pro Bowls and won both. When he left coaching, he had the third best record among active coaches, behind only Don Shula and Tom Landry. He later became a non pareil network radio and TV commentator. Another pro champion coach, Greg Popovich of Indiana Harbor and Merrillville, led San Antonio to the 1999 NBA title. And Gary's Charlie Finley built and owned a powerhouse baseball team in Oakland that won the World Series three straight years. *Photo courtesy of the Calumet Regional Archives of Indiana University Northwest.*

Ace of Aces

When Alex Vraciu of Indiana Harbor was recalled to sell war bonds during World War II, he was the Navy's leading Ace in the South Pacific. In all, Vraciu shot down nineteen planes, destroyed twenty-one more on the ground, and survived service on six carriers, two of which were torpedoed, two ditchings, and two parachute jumps, as he became known as both "The Indestructible" and "Grumman Aircraft's Best Customer." Twelve years after the war, Jet Test Pilot Vraciu won the High Individual Air-to-Air competition at the Naval Air Weapons Meet at El Centro, California, outshooting all of the top Naval

and Marine pilots in the nation. In addition to Vraciu, other military heroes from Lake County include two Congressional Medal of Honor winners: Hammond's William Gordon Windrich (Korea) and Indiana Harbor's Emilio de la Garza (Vietnam). *Photo courtesy of the East Chicago Hall of Fame.*

NBA Co-Rookie of the Year

Bill Tosheff, shown here as a youngster doing a Macedonia two-step, went on to become co-Rookie of the Year with the Olympians of the National Basketball Association. Arguably the best all-around athlete in Gary, Tosh lettered in four major sports at Gary Froebel. While stationed with the Air Force in Alaska during and after World War II, Tosh led a basketball team that, by the end of 1946, had won an unbelievable 120 consecutive games. He also was the stopper of a baseball team that included a future Hall of Famer. After starring with Indiana University's fabled Hurrying Hoosiers and pitching I.U. to its only Big Ten baseball title ever, Tosh not only played pro basketball but pro baseball. In 1999, at the age of 73, he came out of the shadows of fading memories to become vice president of operations for the San Diego entry in the new International Basketball League. *Photo courtesy of the Calumet Regional Archives of Indiana University Northwest.*

Multi-level Star

Indiana Harbor's Vince Boryla, shown here with his Olympic gold medal, excelled at more levels of basketball than any other mortal. Barely stoppable as a high school star at E.C. Washington, he became an All American at both Notre Dame and Denver University. In between, he was chosen for the U.S. Olympic team and won a gold medal in England in 1948. As a pro playing for the New York Knicks for five years, he was chosen an NBA All Star three times. He subsequently coached the Knicks before becoming the team's general manager. With the expansion of professional basketball, he became president of the Utah Stars in the new American Basketball League and finally top man at the Denver Nuggets, where he was named NBA executive of the year. Along the way, he became a multi-millionaire entrepreneur and philanthropist. Another Olympic champion from Lake County was Lee Calhoun, a 110-meter high hurdler who won gold medals at both the 1956 games in Melbourne, Australia, and the 1960 games in Rome. *Photo courtesy of the Denver University Alumni Association.*

The Greatest Otello

After singing leading roles in a variety of languages in European opera houses, Gary's James McCracken gained stardom in Vienna and Zurich, where he astonished critics and evoked wild cheering from audiences. His tenor voice was an unbelievably powerful one, dark and rich in color and precise in placement, a voice that rose effortlessly to ravishing upper registers. He also brought intelligence and insight to the dramatic demands of his roles. McCracken soon came to be recognized as the world's best Otello, the first American-born singer to perform the role, and one of the most exciting singing actors of the twentieth century. In 1963, he returned to the Metropolitan Opera in New York, and quickly became the Met's kingpin for almost a decade and a half. In the early 1970s he starred at the Met in new productions for five consecutive seasons: in Otello, Carmen, Aida, Le Prophets, and Tannhauser, his first Wagnerian part. The oil painting of McCracken as Otello, shown here, hangs in the Metropolitan Opera House. When McCracken died of a stroke in 1988, his obituary said: "He was the most successful dramatic tenor yet produced by the United States." *Photo courtesy of Jeanellen McCracken Straight.*

index

A

Academy Award, 164
Ace of Aces, 169
Alexander, Irene Levy, 162
Americanization, 16
Amtrak, 48
Apple Day, 88
Apple fest, 47
Aquatorium, 152
Arc Information Technologies
   (Arc IT), 44
Art Theater, 106
August, Gary, 22

B

bait, 63
Barlett Woods, 159
basic oxygen furnace, 42
beaches, 15, 56
Biel, Natalie, 135
biking, 97
birding, 72
"Birthplace of Ecology," 68
Block Stadium, 112
boating, 58
Borman, Frank, 166
Boryla, Vince, 170
Brant, Matthew, 135
Brass Tavern, 152
Briar Ridge, 156
Buckley Homestead County
   Park, 73, 92
Buckley Homestead, 46
Buffington Harbor, 107, 109, 150
Burrell Professional Labs, 45
Business and Industry Training
   Programs, 137
butterflies, 71

C

Calumet College of Saint Joseph,
   136
Calumet College, 136
Calumet Room, 139
Cambrian Society, 128
Campbell, Wendell, 130
Canine, Edwin N., 132
canoe, 60
Carle, Marcia, 8
Carlson (Ahlgren), Mildred, 168
Carnegie, Andrew, 138
Carter, Vivian, 167
Casa Blanca, 20
casinos, 107
Cates twins, 134
Cedar Lake Boat Launch, 58
Cedar Lake, 58, 159
Celebration Station, 115
Center for Visual and Performing
   Arts in Munster, 14, 120
Century Mall, 30
Challenger Learning Center of
   Northwest Indiana, 136
Champion Corporation, 44
Chanute, Octave, 66, 67
Chautauqua, 92
Chicago airports, 48
Chicago Skyway/Indiana Toll
   Road, 108
Children's Theater, 127
Chopin Chorus, 128
Chorus Angelorum, 128
Chulay, John, 165
"Church of all Nations," 25
"City of the Century," 150
Civic Center, 114, 131
Civil War, 118
Clarke, George Washington, 6
Cline Avenue Extension, 50
Cobe Cup, 159

coexistence of nature and
   industry, 57
Cohen, Ronald D., 139
colleges, 136
Collier, Marian, 165
Community Hospital of Munster,
   34
Community Theater, 126
"Confederate Airforce," 53
Coolidge, Calvin, President, 153
Cowles, Henry Chandler, 66
"Crossroads of America," 157
Crossroads Shopping Plaza, 30
Crown Point mural, 120
Crown Point, 158
Culp, Marion J. "Pablo," 124

D

D. C. Country Junction and Zoo,
   119
Davies, John, 9
Davis, George F., 156
Deep River County Park, 87
Deep River Grinders, 89
Delray market, 33
Dillinger, John, 159
dining, 104
diversity, 10
Divjak, Kristina, 167
Dorman-Gainer, Linda, 8
Dyer, 156

E

Earl, George, 145
Earle, George, 154
Earle, William, 155
East Chicago Farrar (female)
   Chorus, 128
East Chicago Male Chorus, 128

East Chicago Pastrick Branch library, 120
East Chicago Room, 139
East Chicago's West Side Junior High School, 134
East Chicago, 148
Eberly, Glen, 140
ecology, 66
Edgemoor, 150
Emmy and Peabody, 164
Emmy, 165
Empress Casino, 107, 109, 111
Ewen, Don, 47

F

farming, 46
federal courthouse, 146
fests, events, and celebrations, 116
finished products, 43
First Baptist Church of Indiana Harbor, 25
First Church of God, 25
First to the Moon, 166
fishing, 62
formal learning, 132
Fourth of July, 119
Funnel Effect, 72

G

Gallery Northwest, 122
Gary Emerson High School, 122
Gary, 150
Gary/Chicago Airport, 49
Gateway Park, 150
Genesis Center, 130
Genesis Convention Center, 114
Genesius Guild, 126
George H. Hammond Packing Company, 146
Gibson Woods Nature Preserve, 80
Gibson, David, 152
"Girl on the Beach," 56
Gleason Park, 136
Gold Rush, 6, 160
golf, 64

Goodrich, Mickey, 135
Gordon, Marv, 122
Grammy, 165
Grand Kankakee Marsh County Park, 94
Grand Kankakee Marsh, 54, 94
greenhouses, 46
Griffith, 154
Gurfinkel, Hermann, 122
Guyer, James, 155

H

Hack, John, 158
Halstead, Melvin A., 160
Hammond High School, 135
Hammond Library, 138
Hammond Marina, 56, 58, 61, 111
Hammond Tech, 113
Hammond, 146
Harmon, Tom, 168
Harrah's Casino East Chicago, 107
Harrison Park, 122
Hart, Aaron, 156
Hartsdale Farm, 157
Heart Day, 134
Heisman Trophy Winner, 168
Heritage Park, 153
Highland Museum, 140
Highland, 153
Hobart Art Fair, 122
Hobart Historical Museum, 140
Hobart post office, 120
Hobart, 155
Hocker, Tom, 8
Holy Angels Cathedral, 24
homes, 26
Hoosier, the, 106
Hoosier Boys' Town, 157
Hoosier Prairie, 69
Hoshaw, Sarah, 125
hotel and motel, 15
Hub Pool, 57
Hults, Susan, 125
Hyles-Anderson College, 136

I

Ideal Section of the Lincoln Highway, 156
Illiana Motor Speedway, 115
Indiana Dunes National Lakeshore, 66
Indiana Harbor Ship Canal, 40, 51, 149
Indiana Harbor, 149
Indiana Room, 139
Indiana Symphony Orchestra, 120, 130, 131
Indiana University Northwest, 122, 127, 136
International Culture Festival, 19
Interstate Visitors Information Center, 142
interstates, 48
Irish, 19
Ispat Inland Steel, 36, 37
Ivy Tech State College, 136

J

Jackson, Michael, 165
Jeorse Park, 56
John Dillinger Museum, 144
Johnson, Morrie, 122
Johnston, Judy, 153
Johnston, Michael, 153

K

Karageorge, 128
Katris, John, 106
Kipta, Edward P., 154
Koch, Jessica, 154
Kosalko, Gayle, 8

L

La Quinta Inn, 103
La Tulip's Harbor, 58
Labor Day Parade, 160
Lake Central Dance Invitational, 135
Lake County Convention and Visitors Bureau, 9
Lake County Court House, 145

Lake County Fair, 118
Lake County Museum, 140
Lake County Parks and
    Recreation Department, 76
Lake County Parks, 46
Lake Etta County Park, 82
Lake Front Beach and Bird
    Sanctuary, 56
Lake Michigan Winery, 45
Lake Michigan, 72
Lake of the Red Cedars Museum,
    141
Lake Station, 135, 154
Lake Street Beach, 56
Lake Street, 32
Lane, James B., 139
Lemon Lake County Park, 91
libraries, 138
Lincoln, Abraham, 155
Little Calumet Flood Control and
    Recreation Project, 96
Little Red School House, 141
lodging, 102
Lowell High School, 125
Lowell, 160
LTV Steel, 13
LTV, 36

M

Majestic Star Casino, 107, 109
Malden, Karl, 164
"Man of Steel," 122
maple syrup time, 88
Marian Theatre Guild, 126
Marquette Park Beach, 56, 140
Marquette Trail, 63
Marquette, Jacques, Father, 152
marram grass, 71
marriage mills, 158
McCracken, James, 170
McGwinn's Village, 157
McKinlay, Patricia Young, 9
Medicine Show, 118
Melczek, Dale, Bishop, 24
melting pot, 16
Mendoza, Alonzo, 135
Merrillville, 157
Methodists, 23

Meyer Castle, 156
Midlands, 156
Miller Beach, 66, 152
Miller Woods, 67, 68
Miller, Ann, 154
Miller, Mathias, 154
Moody, Dwight, 160
Morrow Turkey Farm, 47
Most Successful Woman, 168
movies, 106
Multi-level Star, 170
Munster's Elliott Elementary
    School, 134
Munster, 152
Murad, Ferid, Dr., 162
museums, 140
music, 128

N

Native American, 18
nature, 68
NBA Co-Rookie of the Year, 169
Nelson, Edwin "Eddie," 115
"New Immigration," 16
Nobel Prize, 162
North Township, 16
Northern Indiana Arts
    Association (NIAA), 120
Northwest Indiana Opera
    Theater, 127

O

Oak Ridge Prairie County Park,
    84
Odlivak, Al, 9
Ogden Engineering Corporation,
    44
"Old Immigration," 16
Old-Fashioned Buckley Singers,
    131
Olympic gold medal, 170
One Hundred Nineteenth Street,
    33
Orak Pipe and Drums, 129

P

parks, 76
Paul H. Douglas Center for
    Environmental Education, 66
Pavel Farms, 155
Peradovic Choir, 128
Phil Smidt's, 104
PhotoCalumet project, 8
Piatek-Daniels, Mary Lou, 167
Pierogi Fest, 18, 119
Pine Crest Marina, 58
Platis, Chris, 113
Platis, Jim, 166
Podiecki, Lynn, 134
popular amusements, 115
promenade, 56
Prusiecki, Ed, 106
pumpkin festival, 117
Purdue University/Calumet, 136

Q

quality of life, 26

R

Radisson Hotel at Star Plaza, 98
rail links, 49
Ramada Inn and Dynasty
    Conference Center, 105
Ray P. Gallivan Field, 113
"Reader," 122
recreation, 54
religion, 22
Reynolds, Frank, 164
Robert A. Pastrick Marina, 58, 61
Robinson, Solon, 145, 158
Rockefeller, Bobo, 160
Ross, Jerry, 159
Rudzinski, Richard D. "Dick," 9

S

sailing, 13, 59
Saints Constantine and Helen
    Cathedral, 12
Scherer, Nicholas, 156
Schererville, 156
Scholl, Dr., 159

Schweizter, Art, 8
Scoring Champ, 167
Senovic, Lee, 122
Shearer, Joanna, 8
shopping, 30
sinter plant, 42
six-stand tandem mill, 43
slab crane, 42
Slovaks, 21
South Shore, 14, 49, 50
Southlake Mall, 30
St. Francis Xavier shrine, 154
St. John the Baptist Church, 21
St. John, 158
St. Joseph's, 23
St. Margaret Mercy Hospital and
  Health Care Centers, 34
Stallbohm Inn, 153
Standard Oil (BP Amoco)
  refinery, 148
Star Plaza, 100
Steel Coast, 146
Stoney Run County Park, 97
Stram, Hank, 168
Super Bowl Champ, 168
swimming, 56

T
TCI cable, 53
technology, 36
Teibel's, 104, 157
Temple Beth'el, 22
Temple Israel, 22
The G. H. Hammond Company,
  36
The Greatest Otello, 170
"The Jackson 5," 165
"The Magic City," 150
The Ridge, 152
The Times, 8, 52
"Theater At The Center," 126
theater, 126
Three Floyds, 45
Three Rivers County Park, 96
Top of the Charts, 167
Tosheff, Bill, 169
Town (theater), 106

Tradewinds Rehabilitation
  Center, 34
Transportation Center, 51
tropical island, 102
Trump Casino, 107, 108
Turkey Creek Golf Course, 86
"Twentieth Center Wonder," 149
Twin Towers, 157

U
U.S. Steel Supervisors' Club, 65
U.S. Steel, 36
ultimate melting pot, 149

V
Vechey, Bridgett, 154
Village Shopping Center, 30
Virtuoso, 162
voyageurs, 95
Vraciu, Alex, 169

W
waterfall, 102
waterpark, 90
"way of the cross," 24
Weismuller, Johnny, Tarzan of
  the Movies, 159
wellness, 34
Wells Street Beach, 56
West Beach, 63
Whihala Beach County Park, 78
Whiting Baptist Church, 22
Whiting/Robertsdale, 148
Wicker Memorial Park, 153
Wicker Park Social Center, 64
Wicker Park, 65
Wiggins, Jeremiah, 157
wild flowers, 71
wind surfing, 58
Wirt, William A., Dr., 132, 151
WJOB, 53
Wolf Lake, 74
Wood's Mill, 88
Woodmar Country Club, 64
Woodmar Mall, 30
World's Champion, 165

World's Junior Champion, 167
World's Top Masters, 166
Worley, Jo Anne, 160
Wright, Orville, 67
Wright, Wilbur, 67
WYIN, Channel 56, 53

Z
Zale, Tony, 165
Zic, Zivko, 124

about the author

Archibald McKinlay has written more history of Lake County than anyone has, although he usually does so with a twist. His Sunday "Calumet Roots" column in *The Times* (based in Munster) has been running since 1981 and is a bemused look at the saints and sinners of the past. Because readers clip the column and send it to expatriates throughout the world, he has perhaps the widest readership of anyone who has ever written about the Calumet Region. These columns have been collected in a series of books with the overall title: *Duh Reejin, A Workaday Mythology.*

Archibald McKinlay.
Times photo by John Smierciak.

In the present book, the author has stepped away from his usual role as wry observer of scenes gone by to become an observer of Lake County in a new millennium. While he provides some historical context, his view is principally a contemporary one, in which he finds a county that is totally unlike anything he has found in the past.